Living with Purpose and Integrity

Living with Purpose and Integrity

Tom Owen-Towle

Flaming Chalice Press™
Santa Barbara, CA
Tel: (619) 933-1121
Website: www.tomo-t.com

Copyright © 2025 by Tom Owen-Towle

All rights reserved. No part of this book may be reproduced or transmitted in any form or by any means, electronic or mechanical, including photocopying, recordings, or by any information storage and retrieval system, without written permission from the author, except for the inclusion of a brief quotation in a review.

10 9 8 7 6 5 4 3 2 1
First English Edition 2025

ISBN 13: 979-8-218-72648-5
Library of Congress CIP Number: 2025908321

Cover and book design by DynamicBookDesign.com

Dedication

*This book is dedicated to my life-partner,
Carolyn Sheets Owen-Towle, of 50 years,
who completed her earthly journey
on October 23, 2023 ...
in the very midst of this book's creation.*

Rest in peace and power, our dearly beloved!

"The Ten Commandments are not rules to restrict us, but a framework that makes freedom possible."
—Rabbi Jonathan Sacks

Table of Contents

Dedication v
Foreword ix
Prologue xiii
Introduction 1

Chapter I   Focus Upon Your Ultimate Reality 17
"You shall have no other Gods before me."

Chapter I   Beware of Worshipping Images and Idols 41
You shall not make for yourself any graven image or any likeness or anything that is in heaven above ..."

Chapter II   The Eternal Remains a Mystery 55
"You shall not take the name of the Lord your God in vain ..."

Chapter IV   The Path and Power of Slowth,,,,,,,,,,,,,,,,,,,,,,,,,,,,,,,71
"Remember the sabbath day to keep it holy ..."

Chapter V   **Value Your Primal Bond** 97
"*Honor your father and your mother, that your days may be long in the land which the Lord your God gives you ...*"

Chapter VI   **Essential Sanctity of Life** 115
"*You shall not kill ...*"

Chapter VII   **Treat All Relationships Respectfully** 139
"*You shall not commit adultery ...*"

Chapter VIII **Robbery Diminishes Everybody** 161
"*You shall not steal ...*"

Chapter IX   **Seek, Find, Face, Tell, and Do the Truth** 183
"*You shall not bear false witness against your neighbor ...*"

Chapter X   **Cling to Naught** 205
"*You shall not covet your neighbor's house, your neighbor's wife, or manservant, or maidservant, or ox, or ass, or anything that is your neighbor's*

Epilogue 223
Afterword 233
About the Author 237

Foreword

The commandments are like signposts:
They don't grant you the destination,
but they guide you toward it.
—C. S. Lewis

Grab a glass of lemonade or a mug of tea and find a comfy spot. Settle in for a conversation with your favorite pastor, the one who always has time to chat no matter how busy they are, the one who cares about your struggles, the one who listens kindly even when they disagree.

Tom Owen-Towle is one of those pastors. He wants to bring the Ten Commandments "up to date," to demonstrate their abiding relevance for skeptics and believers alike. He aims to add moral fiber to our cultural diet, and to challenge those who assume they obey these instructions when they haven't actually given them much thought.

Tom has been thinking about them a lot recently—and finds that they weave through every aspect of our lives. Not afraid to be vulnerable, to reveal his own missteps, he shares slivers of his story to inspire our own honest reckoning. The questions he asks at the end of each chapter are prompts for personal reflection, but they feel like invitations to sit down with him on the porch to talk about things that matter most. "Tell me more," he'll say as he leans in to listen with his whole heart.

True to the Unitarian Universalist spirit, Tom has drawn wisdom from every conceivable source to get the conversation going. And acutely aware that his own interpretive tradition is not the only one to grapple with what the sacred text comes to teach, Rev. Owen-Towle invited a rabbi (me) to write the foreword.

What does it mean to share a Scripture—not only with those inside our religious community, but also with people of diverse life-stances? We don't agree on interpretation, or even how to count the Ten. What Protestants see as prologue, Jews view as foundational: *I am YHWH your God, who brought you out of the land of Egypt, out of the house of slavery*. It is Word One, the first of the commandments.

How can that be, when it doesn't actually command anything? An ancient midrash on the Book of Exodus suggested it was similar to a king who didn't want to pass any laws until the people had accepted him as their ruler. Who is this God to tell us what to do? Creator of the universe seems like a compelling resumé item, but liberator of the people makes it personal.

It begins with relationship. The Chasidic masters knew this when they reimagined the etymology of *mitzvah*. In place of the Hebrew word for commandment, they associated it with the Aramaic root that means attachment, companionship, joining together. *I am…your God*.

And because God has not yet concluded all the liberation that humankind needs, we have work to do together. Thus, we need the other 9 (or—as Jewish medieval tradition tried to count *all* the commandments in Torah—the other 612) commandments.

Roman Catholic tradition bundles the instructions about monotheism and idolatry as one commandment, and then divides those that relate to coveting—distinguishing between coveting people and property.

Owen-Towle's model for learning, however, reminds us that we don't need to argue about the numbering; instead, we can recognize that each reading adds new insight. He fosters dialogue between interpretive communities.

So where would Tom and I disagree in our exploration of the Ten, and what might we learn from each other in the process? Let's take #6 as an example. Jewish tradition generally translates the commandment as "*You shall not murder*" rather than the rendering included in this volume, "*You shall not kill.*" Rabbinic texts stew a bit over the distinction to discern the best course of action in impossible situations, and Tom is similarly drawn to liminal questions—so we could drink deeply from our collective wells of wisdom.

It might get a little stickier when Owen-Towle mentions abortion in this context. Since Jewish tradition doesn't identify the embryo or fetus as a person, I would likely push back. Laws that presume personhood from conception, now enacted in multiple states, seriously compromise religious freedom for Jews. I wouldn't want to fuel the assumptions that erase such diversity. Yet I respect that Tom is grappling with the ways our values come into conflict, including his commitment to reproductive justice alongside the sanctity of all living things.

And I appreciate how he extends the commandment to consider all the ways in which we do harm to one another and to other aspects of creation. After all, the rabbis of Late Antiquity taught that even publicly embarrassing someone is forbidden by this command, since the blood pouring through their face reveals the emotional violence we have inflicted.

Points of disagreement become opportunities to understand. "Tell me more," we could say—so different than the strident discourse that passes for public conversation these days. Conversation without listening is a mirage.

Tom has been listening, and paying attention, and learning from everyone. He shares these snippets of wisdom with contagious enthusiasm. Each new discovery ignites such joy and wonder; he cannot help but hand it over to see if you delight in the same way. I hope you do.

Rabbi Rachel S. Mikva, Ph.D.
Rabbi Mikva is the author of *Dangerous Religious Ideas: The Deep Roots of Self-Critical Faith in Judaism, Christianity, and Islam* and editor of *Broken Tablets: Restoring the Ten Commandments and Ourselves.*

Prologue

... do the work and you'll find the spirit.
—Isaiah 58:10

My ever-watchful Mother Mary intuited that her shy, yea withdrawn, squirt of a son might benefit from a pad and pencil on the bed stand ... to scrawl stuff. So, she did just that, saying: "Tommy, after your bedtime prayers or when you wake up in the morning, write down thoughts or feelings on to this pad. Dear son, it's yours to use anytime you want to share something from your heart!"

And, slowly but surely, I got right to work!

What might one label this nascent practice: a habit, an obsession, an unremitting mania, or a "positive addiction," to employ psychologist William Glasser's favorable phrase? Whatever the term, this yen arrived early and has stuck as my main mode of traipsing through the world, of "con-*solid*-ating" my scattered emotions and notions, of cornering life's zaniness. I resonate with author Brian Doyle's (1956-2017) perspective:

> *Some of us build houses, companies, reputations, or tribes of children; some of us make small essays in small rooms. Thrashing toward light with a sharp pen is what writers do.*

These small pads are long since gone ... but, lo and behold, the practice persists! Here I am, 83-years-old and composing mainly on the computer (above the garage in a cubbyhole I call "my altar in the attic") but also scribbling in notebooks I carry on my person. Eating at a restaurant, taking a road trip, schmoozing with family or friends, waiting in a doctor's office, viewing a major league baseball game, zooming, or sitting in the pew at a worship service, I'm always accompanied by pen and notepad.

Writing remains one of my chief enthusiasms, along with singing, discoursing, sauntering, and performing magic. It has never done harm or burdened our family wallet. And whereas I'll likely, sooner rather than later, close shop on out-of-town, speaking gigs, I don't anticipate ever shutting the door on scripting. If I'm lucky, I'll end my existence, with a jotter and writing utensil nearby... cogent enough to scratch out something for somebody ... or only for myself.

And if either hand or mind should happen to fail, then may my voice croon or hum a melody that satisfies my soul.

Since 1986, I've been blessed to have composed a couple dozen books and am daily feeding both my computer journal *and* family scrapbook ... 2850 pages and growing. I frequently muse who (either inside or outside our beloved clan) might be interested in perusing my ruminations and recollections, quotes and notes ... often quite personal? And if nobody proves curious, then who might be the one to clean out my computer and file cabinets and cart off my creations to the dump? Of course, it doesn't really matter, does it, after my cremains are scattered in the canyon behind our Church in San Diego?

But, as of this morning, I'm not done birthing. As my spiritual forebear, e. e. cummings, phrased it: "we can never be born enough." Words keep gestating, flopping about, and tumbling forth. In writing, I pay profound homage to my father-in-law, Millard Owen Sheets, who supported, both with energy and money, the publication of my first book and who was still sketching during his final laps on the planet. Of course, Sheets was an artistic genius from childhood to death and the creator of some 6,000 paintings. I'm a grinder—an unrepentant wordsmith—who can't help jotting.

I've recently produced essays in two books edited by colleagues as well as completed, during the pandemic lockdown, what I thought would be my final book: *Making Peace with Our Own Death* (2021). But no such fortune; here I sit, cushioned in my office above the garage, with a heating pad around my waist to ease periodic back pain, bountiful of thought and authoring away, not as an academic but as a pastor, imparting from my heart straightway to yours.

Unfinished.

And for some weird reason, I've fixated on bringing the Ten Commandments up to date! Like some of you, I memorized them in Sunday school, spouted them when called upon, and studied them during my seminary training. But throughout the course of my 58 years of parish ministry, I pretty much ignored them, although I've unearthed in my preaching files, two sermons on the *Ten*: one back in 1978 and the other in 1997.

Invariably, I've resorted to other sacred guidelines, such as the Native American earth-centered mandates, Jordan B. Peterson's *12 Rules for Life: An Antidote to Chaos* (2018), or drafted versions of my own principles for usage in talks and workshops.

Then, by happenstance, a few years back, I delivered a spanking new homily on the Ten Commandments that was personally transformative and led to my conducting a mountain retreat series. But why do I want to reassess them now ... when I'm meandering down my homestretch? Why is tussling with this Decalogue on my spiritual bucket-list? Why am I possessed to sleuth their relevance for skeptical believers as well as for an American culture in need of a respectable and useful canon to correct our wayward character and wobbly conduct?

I understand why I'm still writing: I'm honoring my mother's early spark *and* my own inner imperative. Writing will always be my primary means of communication and constitutes who I am and what I do. It's my foremost meditative practice ... my core spiritual discipline. I reflect and write; I write and reflect ... thoughtfully and tenderly homeward.

Recently, my therapist friend, upon learning about my latest book project, playfully pondered: "Tom, I'm truly mystified as to why you, a bona fide geezer, have chosen to tackle a 3500-year-old document such as the *Ten Commandments*! I mean, in your 84th year? What's up, why?"

"I'm honestly not sure why, Doug; I can only invite you to read along with me, and let's find out ... together."

Introduction

*Where there is no vision,
the people will perish.*
—Proverbs 29:18

There are few modern-day citizens who wouldn't concede that our central crisis is one of meaning and purpose. One poll found 78% of Americans "dissatisfied with moral values these days." The percentage swells by the month.

We're frustrated by a constipated Congress, rampant racism, gun violence, economic inequalities, surging warfare, and bribery in high places, the decline of democracy as well as civility, global terrorism, and environmental destruction. We desire guidelines to reform a culture beset by greed and divisiveness, falsehoods and bigotry.

Internationally, the USA ranks 125th regarding literacy. Astoundingly, 54% of Americans between 16 and 74 years of age read below a sixth-grade level. And our child poverty rate has risen to 20%, a situation that Senator Cory Booker rightly calls "moral violence."

Furthermore, the United States classifies as a world leader in murder, juvenile crime, imprisonment, divorce, production of pornography, and drug consumption. We hunger for a principled moral compass beyond either stiff conservatism or lax liberalism.

And to complicate matters: organized religion—society's traditional backbone—is shaky today, suffering in the worst ways. Nicholas Kristof (1959-), American journalist and political commentator, in the *New York Times* (August, 2023) puts the fate of Christianity in perspective:

> *The United States remains an unusually pious nation, but Pew reports that 63 percent of American adults identify as Christian, down from 78 percent in 2007. If this trend continues, by the mid-2030's, fewer than half of Americans may identify as Christian.*

Analysts suggest that the main reason folks are leaving congregational life isn't that they're losing belief in God so much as losing confidence in the behavior and guidance of religious leaders. Numerous believers have suffered some sort of religious trauma, feel betrayed or forsaken, and quiver in need of healing. Also, according to a 2019 General Social Survey, in the United States, "*Nones*" (those of no religious affiliation) are the fastest-growing group, having increased to 23.1%.

My own persuasion, Unitarian Universalism (historically rooted in the Judeo-Christian heritage), has been declining in membership, morale, money, and in supply of ministers.

Unquestionably, existing religion needs to discover innovative ways and means to rekindle its communal spirit and restore its moral integrity. Our world seeks clear-sighted visionaries. The European

Green party says of itself: "We aspire to be neither left nor right but out front." In wrangling anew with the Ten Commandments, we're summoned to incorporate the vision of both *eagles*, that view the overall landscape from afar, and *mice*, that experience details at ground-level. As visionaries we dare to pull one another out of ruts, spurring kin beyond mediocrity or hedonism toward laudable destinations. We aim to live ethically and spiritually "out front!"

I was recently inspired by the wisdom offered by the coordinator of a program where I'm companioning children-at-risk (and, friends, what child isn't at sizable risk in today's world?). She said:

Each of you adults who are mentoring these youngsters needs to be a visionary—a person who sees ahead, who envisions what might be, and who focuses steadfastly upon life's potential.

You each represent a face and a force that these children wouldn't otherwise see. Your job is to nudge them in directions they might not otherwise go. Never forget that you are visionaries for your younger buddies!

Visionaries are dreamers blessed with a staunch work ethic and a buoyant spirit. Naturally, visionaries will flub up and fall short, but they stay on their chosen path. The visionary prompts us to negotiate comebacks, to be born again and again and again. Our human dignity lies neither in innocence nor in despondency but in new beginnings, in being scarred and healed a thousand times, becoming seasoned and gnarled questors.

Truly, America needs a vision and abundant visionaries, lest we perish as a people. Where might we start? Well, alongside the *8 fold path* of Buddhism, the *5 pillars* of Islam, the *3 gates* of Sufism, the Confucian *Analects*, and Christianity's *Sermon on the Mount*, surely one place to launch a multi-religious forum is by utilizing the *Ten Commandments*. This timeless Decalogue forms the basis of Jewish law and remains of historical power and pertinence for most members of Western civilization, be they believers or skeptics or as many of us might self-ascribe: skeptical believers.

Historian Mark Rooker couches it tellingly in *The Ten Commandments: Ethics for the 21st Century* (2010):

> *No other document has had such a great influence on Western culture. The two greatest rulers of medieval Europe, Charlemagne of the Franks (742-814) and Alfred the Great of England (840-899), both established legal systems based on biblical laws that included the Ten Commandments.*
>
> *And John Adams (1735-1826), American founding father and second president of the United States, wrote: "As much as I love and admire the Greeks, I believe the Hebrews have done more to enlighten and civilize the world. Moses did more than all of their legislators and philosophers."*

Throughout the generations, the Ten Commandments have become a source of both inspiration and controversy, whether in sacred literature, Supreme Court verdicts, or movies. Yet, less than ½ of all Americans can name any more than four of the commandments. Furthermore, in today's ethical discourse, the Ten are essentially taken-for-granted or shelved, deemed archaic or platitudinous. And, for some folks, "God's rules" can lead to legalistic and guilt-ridden lives.

Rather than remaining an under-appreciated set of useless laws or a brittle artifact, I contend, when caringly re-imagined, that the Ten Commandments can nourish both our inner spirit and our outer conduct. They aren't just germane directives for the generation of Moses; they speak compellingly to our eon as well. The Ten Commandments can help provide a coherent framework for a better world—yea, our modern world. The Ten, creatively scrutinized, present classic truths that never go out of style or value! They can furnish a sorely needed moral compass for the direction and sustenance of our daily lives.

Rabbi Rami Shapiro (1951-) informs us that the phrase "ten commandments" isn't found anywhere in the Torah. Judaism actually refers to them as Ten Sayings or Utterances spoken by God at Mount Sinai, or described as the "ten pearls" in the Midrash, and they're offered as principles not laws. Accordingly, we contemporary pilgrims are encouraged to treat them as life-challenges or reminders rather than inflexible decrees and revision them for our own epoch. I'll still refer to them as "commandments" or the Ten, for familiarity's sake.

Before we dig further into their relevance, one can hardly ignore the Ten's convoluted start. Biblical students conventionally tout "the patience of Job" displayed, by this righteous servant, during times of immense trouble and difficulty, but the rocky delivery of the Ten Commandments similarly tested the forbearance of both Moses and Yahweh.

The scriptural account has Moses climbing up to the top of the mountain, disappearing into the cloud that still covered its peak. There Moses remained for 40 days and 40 nights, communing with Yahweh, who proceeded to pronounce the Ten Commandments.

At the end of this session, God gave Moses two tablets of stone, on which were inscribed "the law and the commandment … written with the finger of God." (Exodus 24:12; 31:18)

Lo and behold, when Moses descended from the heights, he was met with revolt amongst the Israelites, who nostalgically yearned for the predictability they had experienced in Egypt. Freedom, after all, is accompanied with uncertainty. It can prove unsettling, even scary. Freedom arrives as both a blessing and a burden.

So, Moses angrily smashed the two tablets. But after another 40 days on the mountain-top, God inscribed and trusted Moses, once again, with new ones. Without this spiritual bounce-back, both divine and human, the Ten would have never reached the Israelites, let alone the family of humankind. Thus, one could readily make a case for an 11th commandment: "thou shalt demonstrate resilience" as exemplified by both Yahweh and Moses!

Each commandment appears in the second person singular, *you* or *thou*, therewith presenting tests for the thought and behavior of us as private individuals. The ancient rabbis even underscored that when God revealed at Sinai, every Israelite was greeted by a ministering angel who set a crown on their head. Thus, the Ten Commandments symbolize a sort of coronation, establishing us as the rulers in our own realm. In the final analysis, we're self-governing creatures, and these commandments abet the job of ensouling our highest selves.

Furthermore, the Ten Commandments were given directly to every Israelite, both males and females, and we'd add today—non-binary and transgender folks—in sum, everybody—without the intervention of intermediaries such as clerics or royalty. The Ten are inherently democratic: for the people, for each of us.

Additionally, they aren't preachments so much as practices, and furnish, when positively and expansively updated, valuable instructions on how to become both wise and compassionate or a spiritually-engaged activist. All in all, how to become a *mensch*: a goodhearted person of integrity, usefulness, and honor.

Crafted roughly 3500 plus years later, this book's enterprise is to verify the significance of the Ten Commandments for our lives in 2025. Whether we take this Decalogue literally or innovatively, all of us would do well to take it *earnestly* as one of humanity's moral cornerstones. And since this book is addressed to card-carrying *heretics* (literally, "choice-makers"), we'll each interpret the *Ten* in our own fashion.

Furthermore, I urge you to quibble with me, as much as you wish, remembering that in Judaism, argument forms an honorable mode of religious discourse. Healthy squabbling indicates respect for your fellow questor. We're summoned to wrestle honorably with both God and one another.

Here's a useful semantic tip for engaging the Ten in our own fashion. Although the overall Hebrew Scriptures are loaded with commandments or *mitzvot*, there is no term in Judaism meaning "obey." Instead, the word *shema*, which means to "hear" or "listen," is used. When we address the Ten Commandments, we aren't being pressured or demanded to do anything. We're, first and foremost, beckoned to listen deeply, then to respond wisely. Our engagement with each of the Ten will take considerable time (as much as we need) and entail the usage of our whole mind, heart, and conscience.

In deciphering the Decalogue for our current lives, I've pleasantly discovered that my own operational values are prominently explored therein: love, truth, beauty, fidelity, peacefulness, bravery, gratitude, kindness, hope, respect, serenity, forgiveness, joy, generosity, and more. The Ten Commandments, when resourcefully unpacked, can awaken the worthiest resolve in our present-day lives.

Author Kurt Vonnegut (1922-2007) used to note with irony that some fundamentalists wanted the Ten Commandments posted in public places, but none of them seemed to wish to do the same with the Christian Beatitudes such as placing "Blessed are the merciful" in a courtroom or publicizing "Blessed are the peacemakers" in the Pentagon.

Now, I'm not recommending that we brashly display the Decalogue on government property as an Alabaman judge sought to do, awhile back, or do as was attempted in Baton Rouge, Louisiana early in 2025 when a "law requiring that public school classrooms display the Ten" was ruled by a federal judge to be "discriminatory and coercive" as well as "unconstitutional." No, I'm ardently urging us to exhume it for the shaping of healthier spiritual and moral lives: yours and mine and ours. We don't need the Decalogue to reside on our walls but rather to thrive in our hearts and shine in our behaviors.

Alas, the Ten Commandments weren't original with Moses. They were brought into Palestine from the Babylonian captivity, then tested and rewritten throughout the centuries, in classic Jewish fashion.

Consequently, it's appropriate to continue this evolutionary process by rendering our own analyses or what is called in Hebrew lore, *Midrashim*.

This volume will furnish cumbersome work for the reader, so let's lighten the load with some humor! Comedian, Sam Levenson

(1916-1980), mused that "different people look for different things in the Ten Commandments. Some are looking for divine guidance, others for a code of living, while numerous folks are just looking for loopholes!" And, moreover, did you know that Moses was the first person to use the *Internet*, when he downloaded the Ten Commandments from the cloud to his tablet? Additionally, liberals tend to joke about replacing the Ten Commandments with the *Ten Suggestions*, but as a practicing religious progressive for decades, I choose to take them both spiritedly and seriously.

Perhaps the most crucial verse in the entire chapter of Exodus isn't any particular commandment but rather the prologue itself: "And Yahweh spoke saying, 'I am the Lord your God, who brought you out of the land of Egypt, out of the house of bondage!'" (Exodus 20:2) All Ten Commandments truly bank on the saving event of the Exodus. Since Yahweh has freed them from slavery, the Israelites are summoned to manage lives of justice and mercy. These imperatives reside in direct response to works and gifts beyond our human doing. Judaism claims that grace is prior to law and obedience is born of gratitude.

The Ten Commandments aren't mandates in a vacuum or demands in the desert. Hebrew religion says, and I would agree, that we should become virtuous neither out of guilt nor fear, neither to impress our neighbors nor to gain a berth in heaven. We lead ethical lives, because we don't know of a better way to say thank you to the Eternal One for the gift of creation itself, for being freed from all sorts of slaveries, and for being loved eternally.

A monk asked Joshu, one of the greatest Zen masters in China: "What is the one ultimate word of truth?" Without hesitation, Joshu responded, "Yes!" The Creation is one lavish offering of prodigal proportions and possibilities beyond our deserving. Life offers us vast opportunities to employ ourselves for mighty, not trivial, purposes. The only soul-sized response we humans can make is saying Yes to life's call for truth, beauty, and goodness. A Yes that translates into yeses where we give concretely of our time and talents to those efforts we cherish. A Yes that enables us to muster the guts to keep tackling head-on the entire Decalogue until our final breath!

The Talmudic tale reminds us that when Moses struck the Red Sea with his staff, nothing happened. The Red Sea opened only when the first person jumped in, took the risk, and voiced a resounding Yes! Existence opens up for one and all, when we take the plunge. I exhort us to take the plunge, by studying the Ten freshly.

Aspiring to lead lives of gratitude, we align our beings with the Eternal One; we remember the Sabbath day, to keep it holy; we honor our fathers and mothers; we refuse to kill, adulterate, or steal from life; and we won't bear false witness against or covet the possessions of our neighbors.

In boldly addressing the Ten, we work, as well as play, our tails off to make the world a bit more just and jubilant, while relinquishing the final results. On my friend's professional desk are four printed reminders: (1) Show up in your life; (2) Pay attention; (3) Tell the truth; and (4) Let go of the results. The fourth is my bugaboo, so I must commit to practicing Henry David Thoreau's sage counsel: "Affect the quality of the day." He wrote "affect," not determine; influence events and meet challenges without controlling them. Hence, I aspire to live in consonance with the *Bhagavad Gita*: "Do your duty without attachment to outcome."

I'm reminded of a Nepalese body prayer introduced to me by ministerial sister Orlanda Brugnola. My homespun version of this ancient Eastern ritual initiates the break of every morn, keeping me on a proper track, as I entertain the menu of my day. This prayer aspires to stretch every limb of the embodied self. I invite you to make your own amendments to my routine.

Upon rising from bed, I plant my feet firmly on the floor, usually following a jaunt to the bathroom. After finding my body's center of gravity, I slightly bend my knees and cup my hands in a receptive mode, right above the navel. I affirm my core with words such as: "I am a child of the universe. I belong here. It's good for me to be alive." Then my hands lift, barely touching, fully stretched to the sky in prayerful gesture, and I continue speaking out loud: "I thank You God for most this amazing day" (e. e. cummings), or similar words of bone-deep gratitude.

When my arms reach their apex, I open wide my hands and shape them into a chalice to welcome the manifold gifts, both trials and comforts, to be uncovered on this unrepeatable day. My words pour forth: "Into my hands are received today's delights and difficulties, sorrows and joys." Then slowly, in circling fashion, I draw my extended hands back to the beginning position, while uttering: "I promise to unfurl these blessings toward every living entity that I greet on this precious day."

I repeat this ritual, perhaps three or four times, to stretch my being in balanced measure and to "affect the quality of the day." After performing this bodily/spiritual exercise, my day consistently tastes better and I'm energized, anew, to tackle one or another of the Ten Commandments during the next round of 24 hours.

Secondly, I marvel that, when the Torah was given at Mt. Sinai, Moses lugged two hefty marble stone tablets up the mountain, not as a well-muscled, young adult but as an 80-year-old elder. Plainly,

I would need substantial help hauling 115 pounds worth of marble, anytime or anywhere. However, I deem it a fair request to ask of me—a fully-conscious, 83-year-old—to realize some hefty moral and spiritual lifting down my own homestretch. How much lifting are you willing to assume, at this juncture, in your own voyage? Moses wasn't permitted to lounge around on top of the mountain but was immediately sent back down to the valley where Yahweh nudged him to start executing the commandments. As Moses's descendants, we're charged to follow suit. In other words, get to work! Hence, my concocting this book.

Here's another, tantalizing tidbit. The number of words in the Declaration of Independence is 1322, whereas the Ten Commandments only numbers 297. Lesson: it's never the length that matters most but the depth of any foundational proclamation!

Now, let's deal with a couple of nagging issues. First off, God could have demanded anything God wanted from us humans, right?

So I'm in agreement with author Katha Pollitt (1949-), American poet, essayist, and critic, who rails:

> *How different history would have been had God clearly and unmistakably forbidden war, tyranny, taking over other people's countries, slavery, exploitation of workers, cruelty to children, stoning, treating women or anyone as chattel or inferior beings.*

However, and this is a critical *however*, God has given humans free will, and, as a result, we won't always make wise and merciful choices, will we? The Talmud teaches that the angels are envious of us because, whereas human beings possess free will, the seraphim have to do whatever Yahweh dictates. In sum, we earthlings have no right to blame anything or anyone else, including God, for the travesties we perpetrate.

Rabbi Lawrence Kushner (1943-) astutely notes: "Perhaps people suffer from hunger, hatred, and war, because God needs *our* help." According to one *midrash*, "God showed Adam and Eve the Garden of Eden and mused: 'I've made the whole thing for you, so please take good care of it. If you wreck it, there will be no one else to repair it other than you.'"

Secondly, my favorite biblical principle is love, and, it's nowhere to be found in the Ten Commandments, although the Decalogue majors in *doing no harm*, the underlying ethic in every world religion. Fortunately, the nearby Book of Leviticus is all about love of neighbor, God, and self, which the rabbi Jesus reinforces in the Christian scriptures.

Moreover, don't forget the Talmud says that Micah's 3 dicta—"doing justice, loving kindness, and walking humbly"—contain all the biblical commandments within them. So, love is well-amplified in both Hebrew and Christian scriptures, even though not mentioned specifically in the Ten.

Furthermore, it's worth noting that the Commandments are loaded with both *thou shalts* and *thou shalt nots*, behaviors and practices rather than resolutions. Indeed, the Ten Commandments are worthy and life-altering, *only* if we perform them rather than merely recite or discuss them. Love is actionable. Or as the Alcoholics Anonymous program sagely avers: "the program works, if you work it!"

Regarding the commandments themselves, the first four focus upon our relationship to God or the Great Spirit, the Ground of All

Being or whatever power transcends our very humanity. The final six center on the horizontal plane of our human obligations. In the Ten, spirituality *and* ethics are married. Hence, a robust religion impels us to pursue equally both holiness *and* goodness.

I'm right in the throes of completing this project, and the high holy days of the Jewish New Year are being celebrated. Rosh Hashanah and Yom Kippur mark the critical occasion to re-envision our purpose, to look at who we really are and what we deeply cherish and bring our identity and vision into closer alignment. Fall is our chance for soul-searching without breast-beating. Now is the season to reset our spiritual core and pursue a biblically-inspired existence. The Jewish New Year reminds us that we've committed personal and social wrongs, yet, more importantly, we're always more than our wrongs. Our shortcomings and sins may taint us, but they cannot define us, because we're resilient and renewable creatures.

There's a painting in a European gallery of the scene in which Faust sits opposite the Devil at a chess table. Faust's face is contorted in anguish, for he retains on the board but a Knight and the King, and the King is in check. Thousands of people have walked by this painting, aware that, in the very next move, the devil will secure the victory. But one day, a chess-master happens by to stop and stare. The minutes change to hours, but still the master stares. Then suddenly, "it's a lie," he screams. "The King and Knight have another move. They have another move. Yes, they do!"

Well, so do you and I; there presents, this very fall, another move we can make ... perhaps at home or work and certainly multiple moves to make the world a better not a bitter place. May this book jolt us to negotiate the moves, minor or major, that we need to make to fortify our individual and communal lives.

There's no greater tribute to human forbearance and fortitude than to see us down, nearly out, then to rise heroically from the ashes. As the Zen poem puts it: "seven times down, eight times up." Or the art of falling forward.

A concluding prompt, before we embark upon our mission. The premier assignment of life is to incarnate as meaningful and magnanimous an existence as possible during our residence on earth. After all, true happiness is a virtue rather than an emotional state. It arrives via our unrelenting effort to be a good gift to the world. The Hebrew Scriptures confirms this wisdom: "Happy are those who uphold justice, who practice righteousness at all times." (Psalm 106:3) Wrestling soulfully with the Decalogue places us squarely on that happy and hallowed path.

The Ten Commandments goad us to address respectfully, make that reverentially, the fiercely taxing and complicated realities of God, Sabbath, family-life, adultery, robbery, killing, lying, and greed. This grueling Decalogue challenges us to face the gloomiest regions of our souls. It charges us to meet the summons of August Wilson (1945-2005), American playwright, known as "the theater's poet of Black America":

> *Confront the dark parts of yourself, and work to banish them with illumination and forgiveness. Your willingness to wrestle with your demons will cause your angels to sing.*

I've found Wilson's wisdom to ring true during the course of my own blemished journey. For my angels to sing, I must fearlessly wrestle with my demons.

Therefore, filled with both humility and boldness, I invite us, one and all, to tackle the Ten Commandments afresh, rendering up-to-date amendments to the *minutes* (literally) of our lives.

Chapter I

Focus Upon Your Ultimate Reality

I. You shall have no other Gods before me.
—Exodus 20:3

Unitarian Universalists have a unitive vision: one life, one people, one world, one God, one suffering, one righteousness, one passage, one consummation.
—Rev. Dr. David Parke (1928-2020)

This initial commandment was crafted during an era of rampant paganism and polytheism in the Near Eastern world, some 3500 plus years ago. The Israel nation sought to be theologically distinct from its neighbors by promulgating a revolutionary concept in religious history—monotheism, which would subsequently become the staple tenet of both Christianity and Islam.

Monotheism is more than a classic theological perspective. It poses hefty challenges for our human behavior. When we see God as one being or an integrated reality—and we humans are created in that same image—our earthly mission becomes establishing moments and movements of unity while still honoring all forms of diversity. We're motivated to produce a united global order, wherein religious, racial, gender, and cultural harmony is assiduously pursued. Ecological interdependence becomes our governing mission in life.

Inter-religious dialogue and collaboration entail rising beyond toleration to establish bonds of conversation and acceptance, heeding the words of the Prophet Isaiah in which God promises: "My house will be called a house of prayer for all peoples."

Eboo Patel, an American Muslim whose cultural rootage is East Indian, at the age of 22, established an organization in 2002 called the *Interfaith America* promoting values of hospitality and compassion. His organization acknowledges that the world is contested ground between "religious totalitarians and religious pluralists." He urges us to choose words over bullets.

Conversely, dualism tends to espouse a philosophical chasm of insiders and outsiders, "us" and "them," as well as the worthy and the unworthy, and can even lead to violence in the name of one's chosen religion.

Rabbi Jonathan Sacks portrays this lamentable outcome in his trenchant volume: *Not in God's Name: Confronting Religious Violence* (2015):

> *The first stage of dualism is dehumanization. This is the prelude to genocide. The paradox in the phrase "crimes against humanity" is that the great crimes are committed against those you do not see as sharing your humanity. To the Hutus, the Tutsis were cockroaches. For the Nazis, the Jews were vermin, lice, and parasites ... a cancer that had to be removed.*

And American slaveholders deemed blacks to be mere property or chattel, biologically inferior to their masters. European colonizers judged Native Americans to be of barbarous nature, justifying theft of lands, captivity, forced removal, and extermination. In the United States of America, BIPOC (Black, Indigenous, People of Color) folks have consistently been valued as less than fully human.

My chosen religious path, Unitarian Universalism, has always been monotheistic, or as Alfred North Whitehead (1861-1947), English mathematician and philosopher, put it: "Unitarians believe in, at most, one God." Unitarianism claims that every *unit* of existence is sacred. Moreover, the nature of ultimate reality is *unified*, and we are mortal guardians of a *uni*-verse.

Universalism believes in a Supreme Being that ensouls "everlasting love." As Universalists we're not interested in our own *personal* salvation, as many faiths are; we're committed to *communal* salvation. Any salvation worth having must include everyone at the table. We refuse to deny another's humanity without diminishing our own. As George de Benneville (1703-1793), an English physician and Christian Universalist preacher, wrote: "My happiness is incomplete as long as one person remains miserable."

De Benneville had a mystical, near death experience that convinced him that Hell was for purification, not punishment, and that, ultimately, all souls would be united with God. He believed that God is absolutely good and loving and would never condemn any human being to eternal damnation.

It's time for a story. In the middle of a long and frightening night, a five-year-old boy woke up in tears. He was staying with his grandfather as his parents tried to put the pieces of their lives back together again. He didn't know what would happen either to them or to himself. When the boy awoke, he called out, "Grandpa, I'm scared." "It's alright," said Grandpa, "I'm here. I'm here." And indeed he was, sleeping in the other bed in the same room, right there, asleep yet alert, listening for his grandson's cry. The youngster heard those reassuring words, "I'm here." But then he said, still crying, "I know, Grandpa, but is your face turned toward me?"

That's the quintessential question of Universalism: is our face really turned toward the newcomer, the foreigner, the opponent, even the enemy? Do we see them as full-fledged, worthy human beings? Or do we settle upon mouthing noble sentiments like: "I'm here, I care." The Universalist tradition calls us to turn fully toward the other, to turn our hearts and bodies toward them in active compassion and respect, to look them squarely in the face, eye-to-eye, with a level glance and a steady gaze.

We live in a world where people are damned in the name of religion, because their views are different, are verbally and physically attacked because their ways of living and loving aren't mainstream, and those of us who believe in a religion of love not hate must offer, then demonstrate, an alternative way of being: the way of authentic acceptance and inclusive compassion!

In essence, Unitarian Universalism proclaims an unwavering belief in the unity of reality and the conviction that love is the undeniable character of that reality. I, as one human being, am animated during my earthly stay to add my own ounces of love to the mix.

Eternal Love is the source and guide of all existence. Our central vow is to love and be loved—deep, all-encompassing, hard-nosed love. As it's aptly phrased in our newly adopted Article II revision:

> *The purpose of the Unitarian Universalist Association is to actively engage its members in the transformation of the world through liberating Love.*

And it's poignantly stated in Deuteronomy 33:27:
> *The Eternal God is thy refuge and underneath are the everlasting arms.*

Moreover, we endorse the passage on Love from the Hindu *Upanishads*:
> *All the universe has come from love and unto love, all things return.*

I often begin my sermons and workshops by singing our contemporary Unitarian Universalist chant composed by Rebecca Parker (words) and Beth Norton (music):
> *There is a love holding me/us.*
> *There is a love holding all that I/we love.*
> *There is a love holding all.*
> *I/We rest in that love.*

One, loving God.

Micah adds wisdom: "What does the Eternal ask from you but to do justice and love kindness and walk in quiet fellowship or humbly with your God!" (6:8) Note Micah, the 8th century BCE prophet, doesn't reference a distinguished theologian's God or some popular deity, but <u>*your*</u> God, literally "your understanding of God."

This first commandment invites us to salute a unifying, transcendent power, however personally envisioned. Each of us is charged to ask what's the name of our primary God? Is it *Gitchi Manitou*, which means: "Great Spirit" in several Native American languages, "Ground of all Being" (Paul Tillich), "higher or inner power" according to recovery groups, or a specific rendering of Goddess such as Great Divine Mother?

I resonate with St. John 4:7: "God is love ... " since, anytime we experience or express caring, we dwell in the presence of God or Goddess. As activist-writer, James Baldwin (1924-1987), affirmed: "The only god worth having makes us larger, freer, and more loving beings." Carol P. Christ (1945-2021), feminist *thea*-logian, likewise emphasized that "Goddess is the intelligent, embodied love that is the ground of all being."

Without getting lost in the weeds, let's briefly ponder the gender of Yahweh. Although God in classic Judaism is referenced with masculine imagery, many modern Jewish thinkers contend that God cannot be anthropomorphized, so any concept of God basically transcends gender.

The Goddess movement emphasizes the kinship between the feminine and nature, honoring female energy for its role in fertility and the creation of new life. Goddess affirmations and practices blossomed predominantly in North America, Western Europe, Australia, and New Zealand in the 1970s and remained a critical force in re-visioning the Judeo-Christian heritage.

Unitarian Universalist colleague, Shirley Ann Ranck, published a pacesetting Adult curriculum in 1986 called *Cakes for The Queen of Heaven*, which examined pre-Judeo-Christian cultures that worshipped the female as divine. It boldly collared the relationship between women's religious history and the personal issues that arise for women living in our patriarchal society. It remains a fruitful course for unpacking commandment #1.

One key challenge in addressing these opening three commandments on God is to identify ways in which the divine dynamism of the feminine and the masculine can both play constructive roles in our depiction of and relationship with the Eternal. For example, although in the Hebrew Scriptures, God is granted the fatherly role of protector, in my own life-experience, my mother was the protector and my father the provider. The nature of our human bonds sways our conceptions of God. How does both masculine and feminine divine energy play out in your odyssey?

Clearly, we humans will harbor secondary and tertiary devotions in our journeys, but the #1 commandment is asking us who or what is the foremost deity or centerpiece of our existence? And how might we embody that conviction of unity in our everyday lives?

The first commandment poses another challenge. Inevitably, we're besieged during our lifetimes with convenient, oft-glamorous deities. We're attracted to divinities that massage our egos and line our wallets. Most of these pseudo-gods make no substantial demands upon us, let alone moral ones. They just make us feel good, perhaps even powerful.

Therefore, as we're crafting our personalized version of God, beware of succumbing to the enticing sins of arrogance and narcissism. Abraham Lincoln warned civil war veterans to cease focusing upon God being on their side, but challenged all to be on God's side of righteousness. And the familiar Spanish mantra: *vaya con dios*, translates as "may you go with God" rather than simply "may God be with you!" Our gods can easily become servile to or synonymous with our wants.

Furthermore, Rabbi Larry Eisenberg cautions: "For health reasons or peace of mind, I invite you to resign from being master of the universe." We can barely handle the daily struggles and machinations of our own lives, so we need to suspend trying to play God. It represents an impossible quest and burden. The forthright mantra urges: "Can you at least admit you aren't God?"

In wrestling with notions of God, I've found it useful to describe *when* and *where* our central deity appears rather than trying to pin down the *who* or *what* of God. Or as the poet, Rainier Maria Rilke (1875-1926) suggests: "God is more a direction than an object." When focusing on where to look for this one God in the crazy tangle of the cosmic web, it's tempting to fixate on familiar haunts. While conceding the richness of well-trod avenues to the Divine Presence, the chore of this first Commandment is stalking the Holy in fresh hangouts, what Thoreau called the "lurking-places of God."

Flexible theists speak with tentative assurance, not cockiness, recalling that God travels incognito, under pseudonyms, and materializes in unexpected places. There are several inexplicable, eye-popping encounters with Yahweh in the Hebrew Scriptures. Remember what happened to Jacob when reclining in what he presumed to be a God-forsaken place and suddenly entertained one of the most marvelous visions of the entire Bible: "And Jacob awoke from his sleep and said, 'Surely, God is in this place and I did not know it!'" (Genesis 28:16)

Yahweh came to Jacob not in the shrine or place of worship but in the midst of a tedious journey and in the prosaic task of setting up camp in the desert. Jacob built an altar right there in a vain attempt to regularize the unpredictable. But it couldn't be done. God refused to be enshrined. Still does.

Theophanies (manifestations of God) intrude in peculiar places and manners. In most God-sightings—such as those of Amos, Job, and Micaiah—the deity is either not described at all or little content of the vision is reported. When Moses and the elders ascend to the top of the mountain, the narrator describes only what is under God's feet. My point is that the Eternal exhibits in ways beyond human calculation and control, confronting us in startling, even disquieting, fashion sometimes, as when Isaiah announced that God was working through the pagan Assyrians to arouse the Israelis from their disobedience. We earthlings must be satisfied with inklings of the Everlasting One.

Let's move on. Two of the most prominent 20th century Unitarian Universalist theologians, Charles Hartshorne and Henry Nelson Wieman, were proclaimers of a serendipitous view of the divine. Hartshorne, who maintained a vigorous mind to the end of his 103 years on earth, was influenced deeply by both his father, a practicing theologian, and also by his mother who inspired him with a simple statement, which he never forgot. "Charles," she told him when he was a boy, "life is big, life is big." Consequently, Hartshorne always expounded a theology that was expansive in scope and vast in spirit. He concluded that God breaks into human experience through the truly novel and imaginative.

Wieman developed a philosophy of naturalistic theism where God is understood to be a power inherent in the universe that "persuades" or "lures" all living beings toward their ultimate fulfillment. He named that power "Creative Interchange"—the universal force that, when enjoined, utterly changes us. Therefore, to participate in a radically open, interdependent, transformative religion means linking in faithful partnership with Creativity.

When Moses wonders how he will possibly accomplish his intricate and unnerving tasks, Yahweh says, "I will be with you." Indeed, those same *five* words, "I will be with you" are mentioned numerous times in the Hebrew Scriptures, meaning that our human journey, at its finest, is a full-fledged collaboration with the Divine. We're summoned to become partners with, not possessors of, God.

After an astonishingly productive 40-year career of serving Yahweh, Patriarch Moses hands the torch over to his successor, Joshua, who must have been quaking in his boots. However, God eases Joshua's anxiety: "As I was with Moses, so I will be with you." And with you and you and you and me, as well, in the centuries that follow.

So, although I've claimed my one God to be Everlasting Love, I would supplement that viewpoint with additional "lurking-places" of the Infinite. As Ralph Waldo Emerson (1803-1882), American philosopher, essayist, and poet, penned: "God is unity but always works in variety." Remember, these findings are only mine. You, the reader, are nudged to tender your own additions and corrections to my theological minutes. I personally pay homage to Buddha's admonition: "Be a lamp unto yourself. Be a refuge to yourself. Take yourself to no external refuge."

So, don't quibble unduly with the choices that follow. My notions are meant to be evocative, not definitive—geared to stir your own hunt for a flock of original god-sightings. Synchronize your search with the sentiment of King Solomon in *Proverbs*: "In each of your ways, know God."

Jewish mystics suggest that the whole Torah is but one long name of God. Scrolls display words running into each other. This signifies that holiness is unified, and, furthermore, that it's well-nigh impossible to disentangle the detections of the divine, let alone spot them all.

SERVICE

Learn to do good,
seek justice,
aid the oppressed.
Uphold the rights of the orphan,
defend the cause of the widow.
—Isaiah 1:17

Find God by becoming a partner in healing, repairing, and transforming the world. Don't look for God, but become Her ally and She will find you.
—Michael Lerner

Encountering God is less a matter of thinking the right thoughts so much as doing the right things. A mature religion strives to major in results not rhetoric. Therefore, our mission is to be concerned about earthly service not heavenly speculation, to be riveted on economic, relational, political, social, and environmental justice more than metaphysics. Jewish tradition describes our true job as *tikkun olam*—"repairing or mending the world"—becoming God's reliable allies in edging the creation toward righteousness.

Psalm 146: 8-9 poses a theological quandary: "Where is God

found?" and goes straightway to the answer: "God is the one who sustains the fallen and feeds the hungry and brings justice to the widow and the orphan." In other words, when we *homo sapiens* are engrossed in compassionate service, we'll likely run smack dab into Yahweh.

Carter Heyward (1945-), American feminist theologian, astutely claims that we're involved in "godding or doing god" whenever we make justice and share joy with the whole Cosmos. The Beatitudes accent the same linkage, when Jesus offers: "Blessed are the merciful for they shall see God." This means that signs of the holy appear in the countenance of those we serve. One of love's trickiest teachings is how to become effective caregivers—whether assisting someone suffering from a broken leg or heart, from a forsaken hope or child, lost innocence or will. We start by recognizing that our job is not to control or cure but to comfort others. Comfort literally means "to stand firm alongside another." I'm not sure, personally or professionally, that I've ever drawn closer to the presence of God than in moments of comforting and being comforted.

Mother Teresa (1910-1997), Albanian-Indian Catholic missionary, was pressed as to why she spent her life laboring amidst the "dregs of humanity" in Calcutta, India, as the questioner put it. She replied: "Well, it's my earthly duty"; then she paused, "No, that's not quite it; it's my joy." Finally, after moments of considerable silence, Teresa blurted out: "Well, to tell you the truth, my duty is my joy *and* my joy is my duty! They're yoked. And that's why I'm a servant!"

In every religion, a sincere, merciful exchange with the stranger is the highest expression of faith. In fact, the Divine frequently comes cloaked in the guise of the outcast, the fool, or the guest.

Love would not have us ask people what they believe or what might be their political preference or sexual orientation, but rather ask their name and how they're doing, really doing. Love bids us to greet one another along life's pathway as the Quakers do: "How goes it with thy spirit?"

STUFF AND SENSES

All the earth is filled with God's garments!
—Isaiah 6:3

While tracking lurking-places for the divine in the world, we would scour a far-ranging continuum of holiness—from humans to other beasts of the field, from plants to rocks to material objects. Immersed in the mundane stuff of the evolving ecosystem, we experience various signatures of God. Naturalists graciously greet animals and vegetation as an extension of God's body or as spirit-guides dwelling in our midst. One only has to read the writings of 19th century Transcendentalists as well as contemporary ecologists like Lewis Thomas and Annie Dillard to discern their unabashed religious tone and substance. Diane Ackerman portrays her mystical sensibility as follows:

> *There are different terms I suppose you could apply to my band of spirituality. You might call it eco-spirituality. I think of myself as an earth ecstatic.*

Henry David Thoreau (1817-1862) put it similarly:
> *We live but a fraction of our life. Why do we not let on the flood, raise the gates, and set all our wheels in motion? Those who have ears, let them hear. Employ your senses.*

Thoreau wasn't a sensually indulgent person deficient in moral pursuits, excessively fleshy. The universe, in its entirety, displayed what he called "the tonic of wildness"—freedom being an intrinsic quality of both nature and humanity. In fact, Thoreau believed only in sufficient restraints to negotiate our social contract. Anything that smacked of physical bondage or emotional servitude was offensive to him. Animals cannot be trapped and caged; neither can human beings, and that goes for the deities as well.

Thoreau exhorts us, as we roam the wilds of the ecosphere, to pay simultaneous homage to the unfettered, even uncivilized territories inside our bodies and souls. He would have us cultivate without taming our inner beasts and unkempt terrain. Thoreau's social activism stems from such mystical naturalism. The reason he spent a night in jail—having committed civil disobedience for refusing to pay war taxes—is interwoven with his commitment to spending 26 months' worth of nights at Walden Pond. In both cases, he was paying heed to the tonic of wildness. Thoreau concurred with the viewpoint of his peer Daniel Ricketson: "I am an abolitionist, because I am a lover of nature." For Thoreau, employing one's senses was a spiritual discipline. In experiencing nature up close, Thoreau felt we were encountering the holy, the transcendent, God directly—body to body, so to speak.

Wonder floods our lives via ordinary things, inorganic objects as well. Author and social critic, Charles Dickens (1812-1870), was widely praised for "his deep reverence for the household gods," which meant that Dickens eyed the marvelous in the mundanities of his everyday life. This appreciation of stuff reminds one of artistic genius Vincent Van Gogh (1853-1890) who remarked that "the best way to know God is to love many things." Note he didn't say to love many people or projects or landscapes. Rather, he said: "to love many *things*." Stuff.

Poet Anne Sexton (1928-1974), in her poem "Welcome Morning," sings the praises of God being present in the eggs, the kettle, the spoon, the chair, and the table of her morning rituals. She writes: "All this is God, right here in my pea-green house each morning, so while I think of it, let me paint a thank-you on my palm for this God, this laughter of the morning, lest it go unspoken. The Joy that isn't shared, I've heard dies young."

SILLINESS

I don't say that God is one grand laugh,
but I say that you've got to laugh hard
before you can get anywhere near God.
—HENRY MILLER

There have been effective ascetics in human history; however, I dare say, the majority of moral pioneers have exuded joy. They've merged activism and ecstasy—good deeds with good times. The effort to redeem the world is serious but never grim work ... or shouldn't be.

One of my go-to passages in the Hebrew Scriptures is Psalm 118:24:

> *This is the day the Lord hath made;*
> *let us rejoice and be glad in it.*

This biblical verse reminds us that every day is a miracle and an unearned gift, to be utilized to our fullest rather than squandered. We didn't make this day; God did, grandly delivering it to each and every one of us. And what could be a worthier response than aspiring "to rejoice and be glad in it" ... to experience joyfully the gift of 24-more-hours, from start to finish.

In German, the word for blessedness is *saelisch* which is etymologically related to our English word "silly," reminding sedate and hyper-rational types that to be blessed we'd do well to become irrepressible practitioners of zaniness. Additionally, the word "enthusiasm" means "God-filled," so as we demonstrate exuberance, our lives radiate divinity.

The *Ramayana*, a Sanskrit epic from ancient India, notes that "there are three things that are real: God, human folly, and laughter. The first two are beyond comprehension, so we must do what we can with the third." In fact, it's via laughter that we're able to make modest connections with God and place human folly in the proper light.

It's time, in our wrestling with these weighty three God commandments, to entertain a couple jokes to relieve our load.

> *Did you hear about the Unitarian Universalist who married a Jehovah's Witness? Their children still knock on people's doors, but they don't know why.*

What does an agnostic dyslexic insomniac think about at night: "I wonder if there really is a dog?"

Know well that any sound religion is willing to poke occasional fun at itself.

The notable Danish theologian Soren Kierkegaard (1813-1855), who explored the depths of philosophy, went to the nubbins of theology when he wrote: "When I was young, I forgot to laugh; later when I opened my eyes and saw reality ... I began to laugh and haven't stopped since." May we modern questors keep on laughing all the way to our graves and beyond, where we just might join a chorus of chucklers surrounding the Almighty.

I appreciate the Russian-born, political firebrand, Emma Goldman (1869-1940), who proclaimed that "she refused to be a part of any revolution where there wasn't dancing." Cuban innovator of "*mujerista* theology," Ada Maria Isasi-Diaz (1943-2012), seconded Emma's sentiment with comparable words: "The trouble with you *gringas* is you don't fiesta enough!"

Playfulness of spirit is not a frivolous or irresponsible luxury, especially given the deplorable state of our union and the universe. We can't afford another humorless crusader. God welcomes laughers, singers, and dancers as cohorts in life's escapade.

The following passage is translated by Daniel Ladinsky, inspired by the 14th-century Persian mystic and poet Hafiz:

Every child has known God, not the God of names,
not the God of don'ts, but the God who only knows
four words and keeps repeating them saying:
"Come dance with me!"

An old Egyptian myth teaches a valuable lesson about joy exemplifying the purpose of life. After death, Egyptians believed they would be confronted by the god Osiris with a quiz that had to be answered honestly. After forty-two routine questions, concerning how the deceased had lived, Osiris asked a crucial two-part question: first, did you *find* joy, and, second, did you *bring* joy?

Note that the emphasis is not on what we've produced or on our possessions, not even on our creative talents or noble works. The objective of our earthly journey according to Egyptian religion is this: did you *find* joy and did you *bring* joy during your lifetime? The petitioners couldn't lie to Osiris, and much was at stake. If they answered these questions affirmatively, they were returned a portion of continued existence. If not, they would be taken away and forthwith eaten by a creature from the netherworld.

It is sufficient neither to discover joy and keep it to ourselves nor to distribute joy far and wide without nourishing our own souls. The ripened person balances receiving *and* sharing joy in equal measure. In being fully playful, silly, and joyous, we experience a prime lurking-place of the Divine.

May we always hold our gods and goddesses buoyantly—with a light heart and a light touch—for God is a playful being. The Great Spirit likely created the world out of boredom, being in dire need of playmates. Through games and song and dance, we're surprised by evidences of the sacred breaking into our oft-bleak lives and calling us to radical amusement. God is definitely about serendipity and silliness and invites us to follow suit. Especially as our lives edge toward completion.

In the end, death's justice comes to everyone to make room for other creatures to birth on the scene. I resonate with the way naturalist essayist Wallace Stegner (1909-1993) phrases life's conclusion, during a mellow conversation with his friend, James Hepworth:

> *I've been lucky. I came from nowhere and had no reason to expect as much from this one life as I've got. I owe God a death, and the earth a pound or so of chemicals. Now let's see if I can remember that when my time comes.*

Truly, we owe—God, this indescribably marvelous universe, ourselves, and all creaturely companions—one death, particularly following a blessed and generous ride. May this debt be willingly and gladly paid, when our turn comes to re-enter the ground of all being.

I say gladly, because we're placed on earth to find and deliver joy. And when our light finally goes out, if we're fortunate, our souls will echo the glorious and comforting passage of scripture from Isaiah 55:12—skillfully scripted upon our Memorial Wall at the Church in San Diego where Carolyn and I were blessed to serve as co-ministers for 24 years:

> *For you shall go out in joy and be led forth in peace, the mountains and the hills before you shall break forth into singing, and all the trees of the field shall clap their hands.*

May it be so, for one and all.

STRUGGLE

The story of Jacob wrestling with a being greater than himself in the Hebrew Scriptures stands as paradigm for disclosure of the holy in the throes of strife. After a night of unrelenting scuffle, Jacob exits with a limp and is graced with a new name, *Israel*: "the one who strives or struggles with God." I resonate with the sentiment of Simone Adolphine Weil (1909-1943), French philosopher, mystic, and political activist who wrote: "One can never wrestle enough with God, if one does so out of pure regard for truth." Being a "god-wrestler," such as Jacob, is a reputable pursuit and a holy covenant. I've signed up for it; how about you?

Israel, throughout its spiritual evolution as a nation, comes to represent a populace willing to rage and grapple openly with God. Cloying and groveling are considered undignified human activities in Judaic lore. "Argue with heaven," as the Jewish phrase goes. Indeed, robust religion has always agreed with Unitarian poet Carl Sandburg (1878-1967), who imagined that "God grows tired of too many hallelujahs." Heaven and Earth weep and wrangle together during life's unavoidable eddy of anguishes.

SILENCE

The Quran famously lists the ninety-nine names of God. But the Sufis know that the truest name is the one hundredth—silence.
—Peter Bolland

Words are wondrous vehicles (clearly, I'm addicted to them), and may we never relinquish them by descending into utter hush. Yet their fragility—indeed, inadequacy—must be acknowledged. The ancient Hebrews refused to write or speak the whole name of God explaining that the concept is inherently unknowable.

The hills and rivers are mute, yet they shout the wonder of deity. "To you, silence is praise" sings the Psalmist to God (65:2) and there is a Hasidic saying: "the altar dearest to God is the altar of silence." And I would add—the *nearest* altar as well. Silence is a particularly potent and evocative lurking-place of God for loquacious types. Garrison Keillor (1942-), American author, singer, humorist, and radio personality, pointedly jests at my tradition: "The rule at the Unitarian monastery is complete silence, but if you think of something really good, you can go ahead and say it."

We Americans, on the whole, under-practice quietude in worship and under-appreciate freedom from work. Our lives are prone to being cluttered with chatter or clapping, are they not? Yet periods of sufficient inwardness enable us to be receptive to otherness: be it the sounds of nature, the sounds of our own interior castle, or the sounds of divine humming.

Pervasive silence intimidates contemporary folks, so we rush to fill our solitude with busy-ness, bodies, food and drink, TV, cellphones, and miscellaneous inanities instead of mustering the courage to embrace holy emptiness. Yet in our wiser moments, we adhere to Meister Eckhart's invitation: "Quit flapping your gums about God ... the most beautiful thing a person can say about God would be for that person to remain silent from the wisdom of an inner wealth."

Entering the silence is a holy vow accessible to all God's creatures—women, men, and children, animals and plants, too. The Greek root *mys* (in the words mystery and mystic) means shutting the ears, eyes or mouth, because in the presence of luminous and numinous things, we're driven to silence.

Befriending the Great Silence remains a hallowed and, occasionally harrowing, adventure for the religious pilgrim. Yet one day when we cross over into the ultimate darkness, we will be spiritually seasoned, ready to connect with Silence as God.

SURRENDER

In surrendering to God, the Holy One or Creative Interchange—label divinity what you will—submission is not required but trust is. Indeed, the Hebrew word for faith, *bitachon*, really means trust. Surrender is about pledging our troth, forging a vow, making and keeping promises ... then letting go. Surrender denotes giving ourselves over without giving ourselves away—giving ourselves to an ally with whom we can play or tussle, as well as labor to co-create a developing universe. Sometimes I call that reality God; sometimes

I don't. Sometimes I choose to talk about it; other times I hold my tongue and simply revel in the embrace of partnership or brood amidst the peacefulness. And surrender implies that sacrifices may be in store for us. Whenever we enter a holy union with either human or divine beings, we do not emerge the same. We're changed.

At the close of our earthly run, we will release our beings back to the Mystery from which we came, from dust unto dust, rejoining the loving grasp of the Eternal One who tenderly brought us into being, has nurtured us ever since, and will never abandon us. "Rest assured" as our Universalist forebears put it.

Study questions for personal reflection and/or group discussion

(1) Describe as fully as possible your one, primary God?

(2) How does God function and/or partner in your life?

(3) Is there a role for the Divine Feminine in your theology?

(4) What might be some lurking-places of the Infinite in your story?

(5) What/who might serve as seductive pseudo-deities for you?

(6) If there is no deity that you affirm, then articulate the core operating principles in your existence? Give each a paragraph.

Chapter II

Beware of Worshipping Images and Idols

II. You shall not make for yourself a graven image, or any
likeness or anything that is in heaven above, or is on the
earth beneath, or that is in the water under the earth;
you shall not bow down to them or serve them,
for I the Lord your God am a jealous God ...
—Exodus 20:4

*You can safely know you've created God in your own image when
it turns out that God hates all the same people you do. God loves
everyone and you should too!*
—Anne Lamott

*Any god who is mine but not yours, any god concerned
with me but not with you, is an idol.*
—Abraham J. Heschel

Despite my brash and plucky efforts to depict the lurking-places of the loving God in Chapter I, Yahweh is everlastingly impossible to represent.

When I was a religious education minister, early in my career, I remember third-grader Alexandra busy with her crayons. Her mom asked "whose picture are you drawing, dear?" "God," Alexandra boldly replied. "But, sweetheart, nobody knows how God looks," the mother lovingly admonished. "They will when I'm finished," little Alexandra answered. A charming story, but the mother was the wiser of the two in this instance.

Nonetheless, as Alan Watts (1915-1973), English author and self-styled "philosophical entertainer," laments: we mortals keep on trying to "eff the ineffable." However, when we enter the most secret heart of the Tabernacle, the holy of holies, we find it to be empty, because no image or picture or sculpture of Yahweh can be made. We may feel the Spirit, hither and yon, but we can never capture it.

Moses, Esther, Muhammed, Julian of Norwich, Confucius, Sojourner Truth, Buddha, Hildegard of Bingen, Sri Krishna, Bhiksuni Pema Chodron, Oscar Romero, Dorothy Day, and myriad others (including Jesus), have been supreme messengers and pointers to the substance of divinity—plus a godlike spark dwells within the most ordinary of us—yet there exists no earthly incarnation that can harness the ever-elusive, mysterious deity empowering our universe.

This means that we are neither gods ourselves nor are any "graven images" that we create out of wood or words, clay or stone, or whatever we wear around our necks or might place on our ecclesiastical altars or car dash boards. The Israelites were prone to worship golden calves, which they did almost immediately after the initial covenant was fashioned. Fortunately, despite being a jealous God, Yahweh forgave them and renewed the covenant. We moderns are no different than the ancients. We break #2 regularly and seek atonement, before resuming our holy quest.

However, let it be known that God, in no manner, opposes human creativity or beauty. In Exodus 31:1-4, our inventiveness is sanctified:

The Lord also spoke to Moses: "Look, I have appointed, by name, Bezalel son of Uri, son of Hu, of the tribe of Judah. I have filled him with God's spirit, with wisdom, understanding, and ability in every craft to design artistic works ..."

God blessed the artistry of Bezalel and has spawned beauty in multifarious figures and essences of animals, plants, elements, and humans. Hence, Yahweh rejoices, whenever we earthlings render our own stabs at originating beauty.

Truly, our life-long mission is to recognize, then internalize, our vocation as creators not destroyers. We exist to leave behind gifts of splendor and loveliness. It matters not whether our inspired response is a painting, a garden, a dance, an afghan, a casserole or some wonder-filled deed.

Our granddaughter, Corinne, is currently laboring as a professional tattoo artist. Her budding vocation is to marry artistic skill with interpersonal compassion in carving chosen visuals on another's body. Delicate and intimate beauty, to be sure.

Furthermore, beauty can be found and formed in the midst of travail and injustice. Henry David Thoreau (1817-1862), quintessential philosopher of nature, spoke of "severe beauty," by which I assume he meant that a view, moment, or exchange may often be abrasive and harsh, but remain beautiful. The manifold expressions of loveliness displayed during our recent COVID pandemic furnish abundant evidence of this truth.

The word "fair" refers to something lovely but also to something just; for fairness yokes the worlds of beauty and equity. As associate Edward Harris professes: "Fair people keep their commitments, give fair gifts, and forgive fairly. Try love as fairness. Life isn't fair, but love can be." So can beauty.

Beholding or generating beauty lights our inner fire. Beauty can arouse the capacity, in human beings, to become better selves. Deeper beauty is known to occasion sounder truth and broader goodness in our lives, personally and communally. Our home-stretch purpose is to embody Plotinus's sage phrase: "those who behold beauty become themselves beautiful."

And there exists no finer way to close out life than with the sentiment of poet Emily Elizabeth Dickinson (1830-1886):

Beauty crowds me till I die
Beauty, mercy have on me
But if I expire today
Let it be in sight of thee.

I personally wear three beautiful pieces of jewelry. I don rings on both my left and right hands, symbolizing, on the left hand, the enduring power and presence of our marriage, and on the right hand, an African onyx/Australian fire opal ring, celebrating my ancestry.

My life-mate, Carolyn, and I have also fashioned a personalized symbol of significance for our marriage, family, and ministerial partnership: a gold pendant which graces our necks. We call it

Growing Like a Tree. This religious symbol is stitched upon our pastoral robes crafted by Carolyn's mother, Mary Baskerville Sheets, and the same talisman was cast in gold by Carolyn's brother, Tony, and hangs around our collars, ever since we were married in 1973.

This prized pendant aims to keep our life humble (grounded in humor, the humus, and humaneness) and in energizing touch with the abiding yin-yang opposites (male-female, internal-external, good-evil, up-down, joy-sorrow, light-dark and more) within ourselves and the universe. It spurs us to honor our roots, grow tall and proud, venture out on limbs, appreciate blessed views, sway amidst life's storms, and resemble the spirit of the poet, Wendell Berry (1934-), American poet and environmental activist: "Be like a tree in pursuit of your cause: stand firm, grip hard, thrust upward, bend to the winds of heaven, and learn tranquility." And, remember, sometimes our life, resembling the tree, blossoms and sometimes it's barren.

While I adore these pieces of jewelry, I neither worship nor serve them. They're expressions of beauty but hardly equal in power or stature to the Eternal One. I wear them to honor where I came from and what I aspire to incarnate during my life. I plan to bear/bare them until I enter my grave, whereupon I've plotted who in the family might sport each of them.

Do you have statues, pendants, sacred altars, or tattoos on your body that depict or encapsulate your fundamental faith? If so, hail them proudly yet guardedly, for idols in the Bible are routinely called "gods of silver and gods of gold."

The reality of God is beyond our crafting, comprehension, and control. Even Moses—the most illustrious leader, lawgiver, and prophet in Jewish history—who lived to be 120 years old, cries out to God: "Let me behold your presence!" And God answers: "No one can see me and live. You will be able to see my back or hind-parts but not my face."(Exodus 33:23) God never shows the face directly, or such would humble, maybe even frighten, Moses. Worse yet, we humans might provincialize the vision; then, stop growing ourselves.

Accordingly, Moses shielded himself from divine impact in the crevice of a rock, where he could catch a fleeting glimpse of Yahweh, departing, in a kind of hindsight. We mortals never get a direct, clean shot of God's face, only moving snapshots of God's rear. But such will do; they must suffice.

There's more. Yahweh evidently likes playing hide-and-seek with us: "Truly, thou art a God who hides thyself." (Isaiah 4:15) This exclamation of Isaiah is repeated in the cries of the Psalmist and Job. The metaphorical phrase, "God hides His face," occurs over thirty times in the Hebrew Bible. Hence, Yahweh was frequently veiled in the scriptures, even to those who trusted God dearly.

In any case, believers recognize that we live in relationship with an absent presence, a Being that withdraws and advances, conceals and reveals. Such is the paradox of questing after God. To complicate matters, when either Isaiah or Paul is having a vision of God, others around them rarely are partaking of it. Humans never share the same epiphanies or mystical moments—the best we can manage is exchanging notes in open company. Therefore, we need the critique and challenge of a beloved community, lest our revelations become haughty or unbending.

Idolatry has been a pernicious and prevalent demon throughout human history. Why is this so? Idols are seductive, safe, and self-serving. Idols distract and derail us from spending our days and nights in a more loving and just manner. Idols lead to cultish allegiance and lure us back into slavery. Commandment II specifically warns against bloated egos that lead to worshipping "representations of any kind." Even ardent religionists can become addicted to our own patterns, postures, and pontifications. So we need to open our souls to self-criticism and monitoring.

Additionally, the types of idols have grown sneakier over the centuries. Think only of potential blessings and curses generated by the technologically advanced world of *Artificial Intelligence*. Beware: the hard-earned treasures of human imagination and intimacy may be diminished, if we turn our lives over to the robotic industry.

Rabbi Rami Shapiro (1951-) recalls, according to Jewish legend, that when the patriarch Abraham was but 13, his father put him in charge of selling idols made in the family's pottery shop. Abraham smashed them instead. His father demanded an explanation. Abraham said the gods destroyed each other in a battle to determine who constituted the one, true God. Outraged, his father said. "You know these gods are nothing but clay. They can't do anything!" Idols, in fact, can lead to vindictive battles and human subjugation. Sometimes, we need to call out hypocrisy and destroy icons of any shape and substance, following the example of the teenager, Abraham.

Nothing will prove more harmful to civilization than humans peddling idols or pushing simplistic and self-serving views regarding God. Consequently, our modern epoch demands our healthiest grasp, however flawed and unfinished, of the human-divine dynamic. As Meister Eckhart (1260-1327), German Catholic theologian, philosopher, and mystic reminded us: "God must be brought to birth in the soul again and again." And again.

And what about the religious custom of "bowing"? Bowing, at its most respectful, represents a serious and commendable discipline. A bow is not equivalent to blind adoration but refers to healthy surrender. In bowing, we let our head drop, we hold our ego in check, and we expose our heart. Taoism reminds us that in a storm, the bamboo tree that can bend and bow with the wind will survive.

In Buddhist practice, the *gassho* or the act of joining our palms and bowing is not only a physical routine, but also a spiritual moment of halting our wild minds and recognition of our human kinship. Bowing means that I revere your presence in my life. I'm not showing subservience but connection. Bowing can be a momentous exchange of energy between two people, as well as a mark of decency and loyalty.

Hence, in my daily flow, I aspire to take four basic bows:

I bow to the needs and purposes of the natural universe.
I bow to the needs and purposes of the world community.
I bow to the needs and purposes of the humans and
    other animals I greet.
I bow to the needs and purposes of my own evolving presence.

You'd be surprised, as I've been, by the beneficial amount of bowing required during the course of an average day. Gassho is gratitude in movement. There also exists the meaningful Hindu practice of bowing while voicing, *namaste*, which roughly translates as "the divine in me greets and honors the divine in you." It signals respect not worship. We can also bow before wildlife and plants, the ocean and the sky.

In the words of Daehaeng Sunim (1927-2012), Korean Buddhist nun:

Bowing is surrendering our physical body and our thoughts of "I". When bowing we should always try to be quiet, humble, extremely sincere, and grateful for everything. Bowing is a spiritual gift directed both outward and inward.

However, when bowing leaks over into idolizing another person or object, it's gone too far. People can prove to be healthy role models, but ought never to be placed on pedestals. Mary Magdalene, who loved Jesus very much, is said to have seen him after his resurrection, and she immediately ran up to him. And Jesus graciously said, "Do not touch me," but the Greek word *hatir* means "to cling to." In effect, Jesus was saying, "don't cling to me, Mary!" The religious journey is the fine art of knowing how to touch life or another without clinging or cleaving, of knowing when to connect and when to release.

Both the Hebrew and Christian scriptures remind us to "love our neighbors as ourselves"—neither more nor less than. There's an implied equal sign in this moral imperative. We cannot genuinely care about others without exhibiting a similar density and depth of respect for ourselves. Our very being is God's gift to us. Self-love is our best way of saying "Thank You!" Whereas we can never *repay* the Creator for the unspeakable gift of our existence, we can and must *respond* with every pore of our organism. Self-care furnishes the litmus test of being an awakened and fulfilled human being.

Integrity has to do with our being integrated, undivided, whole persons. Approaching his death, Rabbi Zusya bewailed:

> *In the coming world, God will not ask me: "Why were you not Isaiah?" because I'm not Isaiah. "Why then do you weep?" inquired his disciples. Rabbi Zusya sighed as he answered: "It's because God will ask me: 'Why were you not Zusya?' and I must face whether or not I've lived up to the potential that lies within me!"*

You and I have everything we need, all the necessary resources, to lead satisfying, not blameless, lives. We have to make adjustments here and there, but eventually we must make peace with the specific self with which we've been graced since birth. According to the Genesis story of Creation, when finished, Yahweh claimed that the universe wasn't *perfect* but "was good, very good." And that pronouncement included us frail, bedeviled earthlings.

Yes, we're good, very good—absolutely suitable for what will be required during our mortal sojourn. We possess defects, all of us, but we're not defective creatures. We're products of the evolutionary process, gifted with enlarged brains and sympathetic hearts that make it possible to understand an orderly universe and to honor its laws. Yet *understand* may prove too conceited a term to describe our actual human conduct. As my scientific colleague, Connie Pursell, muses: "We theorize about the big bang. We perceive the universe is expanding. We've discovered black holes and posit what they mean and can do, but do we truly *understand* the cosmos? Hardly, considering the damage we're perpetrating with global warming and micro plastics and countless other thoughtless and destructive behaviors."

Furthermore, every one of us is disturbed by some demon. Our best hope lies in naming the demon, confronting it, seeking relief, beginning recovery, then remaining in supportive communities of truthfulness and trust the rest of our lives.

I consider myself "a recover*ing* workaholic." It's taken me the bulk of my adult life to realize, then admit, this addiction, which, in part, caused the divorce from my first wife. I lamentably delivered more energy and love as a minister than as a mate. Note I still use *ing* rather than *ed*!

There exists in life both what pioneering Austrian-Canadian endocrinologist of Hungarian origin, Hans Selye (1907-1982), calls *eustress* (good stress) and *distress* (unhealthy stress). The art of balanced self-care is to embrace the former and diminish the latter. But, as we all know, unless there's some tension in the strings, the violin can't play. So, stress or tension is a precondition for growth.

Author and actress Maya Angelou's life (1928-2014) was one of courageous evolution. Angelou advanced from a child who was molested, to a high school drop-out, to one who "created myself" to offer a wealth of wisdom to others through her 36 books and sustained activism. So, even when Angelou writes light-heartedly about ordinary stresses, one pays close attention:

I've learned that you can tell a lot about a person
by the way they handle these three things: a rainy day,
lost luggage, and tangled Christmas tree lights.

Mature persons are challenged to seek a life of ample serenity and struggle. Remember that Jeremiah in the Hebrew Scriptures warned the religious wayfarer that there exist false prophets prancing about, "healing the wounds lightly" and preaching "peace, peace, when there is no peace." Today is no different. There are gurus peddling literature and pushing sessions on how to lead semi-tranquilized lives. I don't want, nor do I recommend, a worry-free existence.

Being well-adjusted means living with abundant concerns, both local and global. Those who systematically skirt all unease or torment quickly turn into zombies. I recommend the sensible prayer of an associate: "May there be peace *and* unrest in our lives, unrest *and* peace"—enough peace to bring us calm and composure *and* enough unrest to keep us morally awake and spiritually on our toes. There's more to address.

Self-pity is one of the most popular, non-pharmaceutical drugs in our culture. Self-pity is narcotic because it gives momentary pleasure and separates us from actuality. It impels us to cry out: "This situation is hopeless; poor me; there's nothing I can do!" Then it becomes all right to whine or wallow in misery. Yet no matter how the fates conspire, we still make or forsake our own destinies.

Self-pitying sorts are forever wishing they were someone else who has more smarts or money or looks. It's self-esteem run amok. It's pure idolatry. As Allan Gurganus (1947-), American novelist and essayist, describes: "On life's totem pole of bargain basement emotions, jealousy and self-pity are the tackiest!" Jesus didn't stand for self-pitying sorts. He was known to have said to more than one slacker: "Rise, take up your pallet and walk!"

Clearly, we negotiate a fine line between mature self-love and narcissism or what Martin Luther (1483-1546), German protestant reformer and theologian, termed *incurvatum in se*, meaning "turned in upon oneself." It's okay to stare at our navels, if when doing so, we acknowledge our vital connection to other people.

We're not sufficient unto ourselves. It is only in the context of community that we become fully human. When the apostle Paul observed that "we are members one of another," he used the word *member* in its original sense of limb. At times, we're truly called to become one another's arms and legs. Lacking one another, we're incomplete, maimed, less than fully capable humans.

I believe this is why the Ten Commandments are delivered not to Moses solely for his personal growth, or to either of his siblings, Miriam or Aaron, on their own, but to a larger, covenanted community, the Israelite nation. The lesson: handling the Ten in a soulful fashion requires the constant backing and review of a beloved community. These rigorous commandments cannot be satisfactorily processed alone. We need to call in our chosen tribe (or tribes) of comrades!

Commandment II delivers one more warning: beware of succumbing to the magnetism of gurus. Only Yahweh is worthy of our worship. We are charged to break free from all the idols that enslave us: be they material or spiritual. Let us continue to personify lives of authentic self and neighborly love, appropriate veneration, genuine bowing and kneeling, while focusing our consummate reverence on the Creator.

Study questions for personal reflection and/or group discussion

(1) Where and when are you tempted to create graven images of the divine/sacred in your journey?

(2) How do you generate or produce beauty in your existence?

(3) Do you have statues or altars in your house and do you wear jewelry or engrave tattoos on your body? Describe what they mean to you.

(4) How do you balance self and neighbor love?

(5) In what ways might self-pity creep into your life?

(6) Is there anything or anyone whom you idolize?

(7) Are there times when you gladly and willingly bow in your life?

(8) Exegete St. Paul's dictum: "We are members one of another!"

(9) What does worship mean to you? How and when do you practice it? Remember, as Ralph Waldo Emerson notes: "... be careful what we are worshipping, for what we are worshipping, we are becoming."

(10) Whom and what might you choose to serve in your time on this earth?

Chapter III

The Eternal Remains a Mystery

III. You shall not take the name of the
Lord your God in vain ...
—Exodus 20:7

The Tao that can be told is not the eternal Tao.
The name that can be named is not the eternal Name.
—Lao Tzu (6ᵀᴴ century B.C.)

God transcends all things and exceeds all intellect
and mind. God is above anything that can be conceived.
—Michael Servetus (1512-1553)

We mistreat God's name whenever we use it to glorify ourselves or denigrate others. Athletes insult Yahweh whenever they pray: "Thanks be to God" after a victory, as if God didn't have more pressing things to do than watch sporting events like I (a baseball and basketball fanatic) do, let alone cheer for a particular team or player. When we humans trivialize God's name to satisfy our own needs or advance our own agenda, it comprises a direct violation of the third commandment.

There's a rabbinical legend that portrays God as chastising the angels of heaven who wanted to exalt him in ecstatic hymns of thanksgiving, when the waves of the Red Sea closed over the drowning Egyptians: "*My* creatures are perishing, and you want to sing praises!" And, Adolf Hitler, in *Mein Kampf*, wrote, while liquidating the Jews: "I am doing the Lord's work!" No deity worth its moral salt ever takes sides in elections, battles, games, partnerships, religious debates, genocides, or in anything!

Moreover, chattering about God doesn't bring anyone closer to the Divine Presence. Sometimes, words can furnish an escape, diversion, or substitute for a real, expressive exchange. I'll never forget the insight of a parishioner who said to me: "Pastor Tom, even though we liberals are circumspect, even restrained, in verbalizing the concept of God, I often feel its presence in the music, the hushes, and the mission we experience together. Divinity is certainly stirring in our sanctuary and courtyard!"

Similarly, Idries Shah (1924-1996), the renowned Sufi scholar, once told an audience after lecturing a full four hours: "Notice I didn't use the actual words God or Love once during my talk, yet everything I mentioned was somehow about these two realities."

Vain is the perilous term here. It means being up "to no good purpose." Whenever we use profanity, we're blaspheming God's name. Whenever we talk glibly or idly about God's identity, we're exploiting the Divine Mystery. It's tempting to wax superficial about God, such as when we pray incessantly for gun violence victims; then we fail to expedite substantial gun reform. Prayer without action is hypocrisy!

I also find New Age prattle about accessing celestial energy, to be the equivalent of "spirituality light." Metaphysical embraces, without ethical demands, ring hollow. The truth is, as the prophet Micah goads, the Eternal One *requires* much of us: "to do justice, love kindness, and walk humbly with your God." Religion majors in requirements.

When addressing the first commandment that "God is One" I tendered my own verdict that God is primarily Everlasting Love; then I went on to explore six lurking places where I find said Love to reveal itself in my life. Despite these bedrock convictions, this third commandment cautions me to remember that God remains inexplicable. God may disclose in omens and hints, but, unlike a mystery novel, cannot be definitively decoded.

Spiritual seekers, including myself, have trouble allowing God to be utterly mysterious; so, we craft concepts of divinity which tend to resemble our own human traits and values ... in sum, the best of *us*! Or we fashion God roughly in our own image to give ourselves the facade of superhuman power and control. However, any descriptions of the Infinite Unknown I've rendered in this book are but personal choices rather than irrefutable wisdom. Dancing with or delving into God poses a chastening enterprise.

I remember, at the start of my ministry in 1970, as Minister of Education, sharing a conversation about God with primary age children in our chapel worship one Sunday. I inquired: "What does God look like?" There were various answers, but the one that stuck with me that morning was: "God is fat!" After the initial shock to my adult ears, I've grown to understand, yea appreciate, that offbeat response of my 9-year-old buddy. Because God is indeed fat, colossal, and mammoth—a reality that incorporates all conceivable human notions yet still remains bigger than that. Fat doesn't do God justice, but at least it's moving in the right direction—away from puniness or a biased perspective.

The *Rig Veda*, ancient Hindu scripture (1500-1000 BCE), refers to the Eternal as extending "ten fingers breadth beyond." The Muslims say "*allahu akbar,*" which means not "God is great!" (as is often translated), but "God is greater!"—greater than any of our earth-bound visions or dogmas.

16th century Unitarian forebear, Michael Servetus, depicts God as being "above anything that can be conceived." Universalist Benjamin Rush in 1790 refers to the Supreme Being as "infinite in all its perfections ... incomprehensible." Late-twentieth century theologian, Bernard Loomer, focused his "process thought" on describing a God of larger proportions than mere abstractions could ever achieve. He kept emphasizing the "size" of God: huge in both grandeur and goodness.

Consequently, I belong to the company of loyalists who refuse to posit a deity that is regionalized or graspable. Hence, a responsibly free faith is as expansive as the cosmos and resonates with the story of Rabbi Moshe of Kobryn who said: "When you utter a word before God, then enter into that word with every one of your limbs." One of his listeners remarked: "How can a big human being possibly enter into a little word?" "Anyone who thinks themselves bigger than the word," said the *zaddik*, "is not the kind of person we're talking about!"

Newcomers are entering religious gates nowadays hungry for meaning and discipline. They're unabashedly *homo religiosus*, seekers of the transcendent. One young-adult member of our congregation recently opined: "I originally came to First Church to foster a deeper bond with God, but I quickly became preoccupied with social issues and various committees. I forfeited time and energy to engage the Holy. It was a major loss! I need to reboot and get back on course!"

A pressing question persists: will contemporary questors and future generations choose to shape and hone their spiritual lives dwelling inside or outside the venue of a church, synagogue, sangha, or mosque? Will they need communal life to gratify their holy impulses? Will they choose to "meet up" in person? Will they be prone to join and maintain institutions?

Nonetheless, the Creator has been getting more ink today than in a long time ... and oft from the unlikely pens of established physicists or adventurous literati. There even exists modern-day medical research that makes the case for a sixth human sense that intuitively perceives the divine. God may be on the human brain, declare some scientists. Perhaps we're hardwired to be religious seekers even if not organizational sustainers.

I pay heed to a religion that pushes our minds as far as they can go and then bows before the mysteries. The primary mystery of existence is life itself, a reality we all share. It's not always fair or sweet or beautiful, but it's a gift, a marvel, since each of us is a statistical miracle. Blessed are those who, rather than either avoiding or explaining these mysteries, have the courage to bow before their perplexity and power, from beginning to end.

Life's mysteries are double-edged; they both attract and repel. Awake and exposed, humans tremble in the presence of the numinous. The mysteries of birth, love, evil, death, sexuality, and the cosmos are uncanny and elicit a special feeling, best rendered by the English word "awe" and its derivatives "awesome" and "awful."

The astonishment we experience in the presence of the Holy is reinforced by the fact that the "ah" sound is present in the name of most deities: Adonai, Yahweh, Allah, God, Rama, Goddess, Shiva, and Krishna.

One approach, when wrestling with God, that's helped me remain humble, while soaking in mystery, is what I call juggling the three A's (atheism, agnosticism, and affirmatism). This balancing act keeps us from sliding into dogmatism of any shape or form. When these three perspectives are clasped in resourceful tension, our religious identity becomes hale and hearty; for each attitude contributes to the theological process and provides a system of checks and balances in unpacking these three commandments on holiness. French philosopher, Blaise Pascal (1623-1662) noted as much in his confessional volume, *Pensees*:

Denying, believing, and doubting completely
are to humans what running is to a horse.

My approach is also akin to that of American journalist and syndicated columnist, Ellen Goodman (1941-), who writes: "In an argument between true believers, I often side with ambivalence. I'm drawn to the ambidextrous one who can argue with both hands." Yes, I can neither explain adequately nor avoid entirely the presence of God. Thus, I argue with both hands as well as with a full heart and head.

Being riders of paradoxes is apparently our peculiar niche as broadminded religionists. We seem to pitch a tent in the creases between holiness and humanism, theism and naturalism, believing and doubting, devotion and skepticism. We pursue a reasonable religion with mystical sensibilities. Colleague Frances West puts it sagely: "the humanist and the theist live in me, each sometimes puzzled by the presence of the other, but willing to keep talking. So, may it continue."

Clearly, there's a danger in either extreme. Arid humanism can trap us in the mundane and material, making us oblivious to trans-rational (note I didn't say irrational) nudges and detections. On the other hand, unbridled theism can swallow humans in the supernal ether, when our paramount job is to make this precious earth more beautiful and just.

So, mystical humanism (what someone has awkwardly coined "*humanisticism*") is perhaps the principal conundrum to harness, then dare to ride. Some do it sidesaddle, tentatively; others with both hands to the reins, galloping, full-bore ahead. Regardless, it provides a spirited jaunt!

So, let's launch our wild excursion with an assessment of atheism which, at its best, comprises a refining influence, eliminating obsolete or abhorrent renditions of the divine. Eminent 20th century Polish-American rabbi and philosopher, Abraham Joshua Heschel (1907-1972) routinely pondered that veritable prophets spend the bulk of their time interfering with and raging against puerile, self-serving notions of the Creator.

Unitarian Universalism is an established faith that contends that religious people can be self-ascribed atheists—be they of the distracted, functional, or cheerful variety. We know that countless human explorers, within and without our fold, have experienced what they might call transcendent insights and moments without attributing them to a supernatural source. They perceive such encounters to be indigenous and natural to this earthly sphere.

Plus, some, but not all, atheists are tinged with a sort of existential regret. In fact, American psychologist Paul Vitz (1935-) studied the lives of several atheists and concluded that many had lousy relationships with their fathers. Undoubtedly, there's a kernel of truth in Vitz's analysis, since rejection by one's earthly father often indicates disconnection from a heavenly patriarch as well.

However, one could find agnostics and affirmatists who have also harbored troubled alliances with their fathers and/or their mothers. I've counseled rabid believers who've felt the overweening urge to turn their lives over to an omnipotent, custodial sort of Being, precisely because they suffered deficient parenting during formative years. In sum, we're our histories, and whereas our theologies frequently mirror our psycho-social development, our resultant conditions are varied and seldom easy to pigeonhole.

I personally find atheism most valuable as a clarifying, cleansing vehicle and least useful when stubborn or combative. Atheism is beneficial when employed in service of religious wisdom rather than as an outright negation of it. The bottom line is that atheists hold many noble and moral convictions such as beauty, justice, and love. And never forget that believing in God doesn't automatically make you a good person. Your behavior does! Many atheists describe themselves as secular or religious humanists. If that or a similar designation fits your perspective, I still urge you to grapple flexibly with these first three commandments addressing the nature of God.

Here's another germane twist on commandment III. When we examine the credentials of the signers of the *Humanist Manifesto* back in 1933, two things are evident. First, most of the 34 were card-carrying Unitarian and/or Universalist ministers. Second, while the designers were neither secularists nor super-naturalists, they exuded an obvious fondness for the sacred. Unlike the orthodox theists of their day, they didn't worship a patriarchal figure high in the sky. Nonetheless, they were notably reverent travelers. They handled holy things with feeling. They were open to the divine circulating through this earthly trek.

These thoroughgoing humanists talked of God, comfortably so, but in collaborative, naturalistic terms. They affirmed some version of partnership between heaven and earth to be their supreme summons. As Unitarian minister Burdette Backus (1888-1955) put it:

> *Whenever we are helping humanity to be at its best, we are worshipping God ... we are the children of a creative and dynamic universe, and its restless energy is at work within us to carry forward the work of creation. This is something of what I mean when I say that I believe in God ... God is not an idea to be believed in; God is work to be done in the world. This work is being accomplished in the growth of human souls, yours and mine.*

Such pacesetters struggled to extend religion beyond narrow humanism and doctrinaire theism. They were both hard-headed and soft-hearted theologians, refusing to exclude or harm anyone with their view of either humanity or divinity. They were inquirers who were agile whether meditating upon the heavens or protesting earthly wrongs. I like to think of them as god-fearing earthlings.

Furthermore, being an honest atheist places one in good company throughout the sweep of world religions. There are clearly nontheistic as well as theistic strands of Hinduism. Such questors are also consonant with the philosophy of Theravada Buddhism, one of the major world religions, where there exists no single, uniform concept of a personal deity. Buddha himself warned that ethereal speculation about the nature of deity or an afterlife not only was futile but also tended not to edification. And as for the Zen Buddhists, when one famous Roshi was asked, "What does Zen say about God," he remained silent.

The high religions of Asia do not acknowledge a personal absolute yet consider the world to be unmistakably numinous. In China, Confucianism is essentially atheistic in that it concentrates on rules of behavior for the conduct of human life rather than worship of a supernal being. So atheism, at its healthiest, dare I say, at its holiest, provides a critical, purifying role in the pursuit of levelheaded religion.

Agnosticism supplies the essential gift of measured indecision, challenging questors to handle the sacred lightly without squeezing it into glib formulas. We can't escape the existential state of partial wisdom. Certitude will never reside within our grasp. "A definite maybe" was the phrase cartoonist Walt Kelly used when answering what he considered life's big questions. The term *agnostic* specifically refers to one who confesses, "I do not know." The Sanskrit antecedent of the Greek contained additional emotional overtones: "to stand in awe before the unknown." The agnostic is fully at peace with unknowability. Agnosticism marks an active reverence and a thirsty curiosity.

Yet the general populace remains oft-confused or unresponsive to the integrity of the agnostic's perspective. British philosopher and mathematician, Bertrand Russell (1872-1970), illustrates this plight in a telling anecdote during the process of his refusal to enter military conscription. "When I reported to the prison warden," Russell said, his eyes changing from their typical gravity to a twinkle, "he asked me the customary questions—name, age, place of residence. Then he inquired, 'religious affiliation?'" "Agnostic," Russell replied. The befuddled guy looked up, "how do you spell that?" Russell spelled "a-g-n-o-s-t-i-c" for him. The warden wrote the word carefully on the prison admission form, then sighed, "Oh, well, there are a great many sects nowadays, but I suppose we all worship the same God!"

Affirmatism unflinchingly insists upon the inherent sacredness of existence, specifying surprising locales of holy portent, as I've aspired to do in Chapter I. I like to think of affirmatists or yea-sayers as explorers, because once we've sought and found smudges of divine fingerprints, we're eager to investigate our discoveries in greater depth. We seekers become finders become explorers in the ever-evolving religious expedition.

The affirmatist maintains that *Yes* is perhaps the central synonym for God. But one huge Yes will not suffice. We must embody affirmatism in the minute exchanges of our daily trek: giving unstintingly of our time, our chutzpah, and our resources. And, moreover, as Dietrich Bonhoeffer (1906-1945), German Protestant theologian and anti-Nazi dissident, staunchly stated:

> *Your "yes" to God requires your "no" to all injustice,*
> *to all evil, to all lies, to all oppression and violation*
> *of the weak and poor.*

William Blake's admonition obtains: "without contraries, there is no progression." Healthy atheism produces a more inventive agnostic, while affirmatism impels us to be more supple atheists and agnostics. Holding paradoxes in sensitive stretch keeps our gullible proclivities from running amok. Alas, when theologically uptight, we're likely to "make premature peace" with either our ignorance or biases.

This reminds me of the humorous account of Schwartz and Rosen, who are strolling to synagogue. Someone stops them and asks Rosen: "May I ask, why are you going to synagogue? Schwartz is a believer; I know why he's going. But you're not religious; you're an atheist!" Rosen answers, "Well, Schwartz goes to talk to God, and I go to talk to Schwartz." You see, a full-fledged, hearty religion can include both human conversation and divine communion, an intriguing mix of Schwartz and Rosen.

Standing tall in the proud lineage of theological pluralism, a contemporary parishioner of ours recently mused: "I first entered Unitarian Universalism as a Christian, evolved into a mystical humanist, and now I'm a card-carrying pagan—and I've never been asked to leave the fold!" Truly, more than a single conviction can circulate in each of us at once. We can become theological crossbreeds in our progressive movement of freethinking mystics with hands. We resonate with American poet and essayist, Walt Whitman's (1819-1892) who claimed: "Do I contradict myself? Yes, I contain multitudes!"

There's more to address. All our words, not only those about deity, matter. Oh, the wondrous power of words to muzzle or motivate, harm or heal. The second chapter of the Bible recounts that God breathed into the nostrils of human, and it became a "living being." An early Aramaic translation of that phrase, reads: "Adam was given the spirit of speech." Through language we become living souls. No group of modern people without speech has ever been found.

So let us use our words wisely and compassionately, every last one of them. And when we do so, we will be honoring God, in whose image we were made. In fact, a cornerstone of the 8 steps to enlightenment, taught by Buddha some 2500 years ago, is "right speech." Living in a world of exaggerated advertising, hate radio, internet abusers, and political spin-doctors, right speech is no mean feat. Yet that's our religious enterprise: to think deeply and to speak humanely; then, to act honorably. Remember the wisdom: one *zinger* (rudeness, dismissal, acrimony) has the power to erase twenty acts of kindness!

And when we have something difficult, even critical, to say to somebody, the recipe is to voice our truth in tenderness. Jesus, in the gospel of Matthew, was asked to sum up the 613 laws of Leviticus in the Hebrew Scriptures, and the Nazarene did so by encouraging us to "reprove our neighbor with kindly and gentle intent." Not to blast or judge our neighbor, but, if we must correct or challenge them, to do so caringly. Our words can injure or damage, and one of the crucial promises within the Hippocratic Oath, as well as within the Ten Commandments, is: "*Primum, non nocere* or first, do no harm."

A rabbi once asked members of a crowd if they could go for 24 hours without saying any unkind words about or to anybody. A minority of listeners raised their hands signifying yes, some folks simply chuckled, while a considerable number called out "no!" Then the Rabbi responded, "All of you who can't answer yes must recognize the problem you have. Because if I ask you to go for two hours without drinking liquor, and you said, 'I can't do that,' I'd have to tell you that you're most likely a practicing alcoholic. So, what keeps us from realizing our addiction to the negative use of words?"

Commandment III is asking us to consider the vow of speaking no evil (or a minimal amount) on a daily basis; moreover, take the time to utter affirmative blessings to ourselves and all whom we meet on life's path. Once we get into the habit of speaking rightly rather than wrongly, it might just prove hard to break.

Study questions for personal reflection and/or group discussion

(1) Are there ways when and where you might talk wrongly or in vain about God?

(2) Do you ever find yourself trying to solve the human and divine mysteries of existence or are you willing simply to soak in them?

(3) What might be the useful gifts provided by practicing atheism, agnosticism, and/or affirmatism? Share examples.

(4) Describe the place of *awe* in your journey?

(5) In what ways might you identify yourself as a theological pluralist?

(6) Name some of the ways in which you discover yourself talking idly, gossiping, or hurtfully, human to human?

(7) What disciplines enable you to utilize "right speech"?

Chapter IV

The Path and Power of Slowth

IV. Remember the Sabbath Day, to keep it Holy
—Exodus 20:8

If you spend a perfectly useless afternoon in a perfectly useless manner, then you have learned how to live.
—Lin Yutang (1895-1976)

The Sabbath isn't a day of prohibitions but of permissions: permission to dream again and restore our soul.
—Rabbi Naomi Levy

There's probably no more important commandment than #4; in fact, it was considered a distinctive mark of Judaism and a brand-new institution in human history. We're directed to schedule times of utter rest and renewal, deep contemplation and conversation in our daily journeys. And the timing of the fourth saying is optimal, coming right after strenuous grappling with the divine and before we engage six stringent ethical directives. It furnishes a consecrated break. The mission of the Sabbath is nothing less than the delivery of essential joy and freedom.

As Rabbi Arthur Green, American scholar of Jewish mysticism and Neo-Hasidic theology (1941-), tellingly puts it:

> *The notion that the entire people, not just the king and the nobles, were given the divine gift of rest, sharing it with God, was one of the great innovations of biblical religion. In the ancient Near Eastern world, only the gods rested.*

Sabbath literally means to "draw a deep breath," without which our lives quickly succumb to stress and chaos. We can draw a deep breath by inner reflection or communal worship, but both quests must be intentional and methodical. Buddhist activist Thich Nhat Hanh took Thursdays off even during the period when the South Vietnamese government was trying to suppress the peace movement in which he was intensely involved. His cohorts cried out: "Sir, they're raiding your office and stealing your papers!" Hanh replied: "Remember, today's Thursday; I'll see to it tomorrow!"

Across the globe, Buddhists practicing in the Plum Village lineage celebrate periodic *Lazy Days* at their hermitages. Monastics and retreat participants seek to be fully present to the day without any scheduled activities. Folks are summoned to stop, sit, be silent, calm, and still ... letting the 24 hours unfold serenely and surprisingly.

Henry Cadbury, the Quaker biblical authority, tells about a small boy who, when asked which story in the Bible he liked best, quickly replied: "That one about the multitude ... you know, the multitude that loafs and fishes." We chuckle, yet the truth is that most adults are rather uncomfortable with the thought of just loafing and fishing. We have difficulty being lazy in all good conscience. Loafing hasn't dwelt in either my genes or my calling, although now nestled in what I term re-*fire*ment, I've been able to partake of the blessings of purposeful inactivity. Well, sometimes.

What do I mean by laziness? I mean a tranquil kind of un-ambitiousness. I mean being able to perch on the periphery of life, relatively unknown, and not always landing center-stage. I mean the ability to empty myself of daily duties, both difficult and delightful ones. I mean the willingness to step aside and step back in order to ruminate and repair, even when bored or listless. As one of my favorite chants puts it: "I am moving on a journey to nowhere, taking it easy, taking it slow. No more hurry, no more worry, nothing to carry, let it all go."

Seasoned meditation practitioners keep encouraging me, as a newbie, to stream with life's flow … as a rolling river. And my recovery program companions remind me to quit pressing to dictate or control the lives of friends and loved ones. These spiritual disciplines nudge me to pursue the arts of letting go, letting be, and letting come. One of my homestretch goals is to become free, solid, and lazy enough to welcome any luminescent stuff that might arise. So, like the Zen archer, I might hit the target, every now and then, precisely because I'm not aiming at it.

Each of us, it seems to me, is about as lazy as we have the courage to be. In a world of consumption, productivity, and status-seeking, lazy is a nasty four-letter word, oft-used for people who defy understanding or exasperate us. Laziness, by definition, means aversion to labor, idleness, even indolence. Clearly, it takes real *chutzpah* to be lazy by choice. Here are three modest tips that have proven useful during my own final laps on earth.

First, be bold enough to come up with a good excuse for cancelling out of a meeting or activity. I recall a person phoning me recently to scratch a promise he'd made. He was both nervous and apologetic. What he didn't know was that I was contemplating using my own excuse to bow out of our scheduled date.

Second, when our life-schedule becomes overgrown, don't hesitate to shear it, or, at least, weed it thoroughly! Plus, while pruning and shedding during the course of our days and nights, remember to prioritize and protect non-repetitive events. For example, there are treasurable passages with my grandkids, and great-granddaughter, that can't be missed—recitals, fiddling-around, gamboling, and games—special flashes of engagement and meaning. Moments that won't come again.

Third, let others serve, even carry, you. Often, our family and friends enjoy, note that, *enjoy*, doing things for us, but we all too rarely allow them to do so. Kick back and learn how to live in the passive voice. Let others take over, sometimes, amidst our haze.

We mortals aren't the only ones in dire need of such respite and renewal. Yahweh takes the practice of Sabbath personally, for in the book of Exodus we read: "In six days, God made heaven and earth, and on the seventh day God rested and was refreshed." (20:11) The word *refreshed* accurately reads, "and God exhaled." Thus, when our human labor is done, in good conscience, we're invited to enjoy a respite, just like the Creator did. Exhale! And, by the way, notice how adept plants and animals are at welcoming peacefulness in their day-to-day hubbub.

Barbara Brown Taylor (1951-) American Episcopal priest, academic, and author expands the concept of Sabbath:

> *Sabbath is not only God's gift to those who have voices to say how tired they are; Sabbath is also God's gift to the tired fields, vines, and land. Leviticus 25 shows divine concern for grapes, for God's sake. It promises both the tame and wild animals in the land enough to eat. It is the great equalizer; that we do not live on this earth but in it ...*

There's savvy contained in the 4th commandment, especially for goal-oriented Westerners (and activist types). Actually, two commandments are melded into one, because remembering the Sabbath covers only half of the charge. To render the Sabbath sacred, it must be *kept* not merely acknowledged. As Alice Walker (1944-), American writer and social reformer, astutely observes: "Anybody can observe the Sabbath, but making it holy surely takes the rest of the week."

I conduct regular workshops for seniors on "Conscious Aging: The Art of Finishing Life Well," and the transition from a human *doing* to a human *being* is elusive. For elders who have ceased working in an official, wage-earning capacity, it's never easy to stop pushing or being pulled by a routine. It's tough to slow-poke during the elective years, when each and every day is essentially ours to program from scratch. Yielding to aloneness, marinating in silence, and keeping the Sabbath are knotty pursuits, at any age, in a culture where busyness and output are equated with human value.

We two-leggeds are hard put to recognize our worthwhileness, unless we're in motion, sometimes perpetual bustle. Yet when we surrender to periods of quietude, we're liberated both in body and soul. Rabbi Abraham Joshua Heschel keenly equates Sabbath with "inner liberty."

> *Nothing is as hard to suppress as the will to be slave to one's own pettiness. Gallantly, ceaselessly, quietly we must fight for inner liberty to remain independent of the enslavement of the material world, free of domination of things as well as from domination of people.*

My father, like so many males of his generation, never got the hang of lounging around without the pressure of an agenda. Harold Alexander Towle (1906-1987) was a creature of his times: a consummate provider who kept putting out and giving forth, while harvesting little of his inner realm.

Dad was able to bless others but rarely allowed others to bless him. His adult-long profession was vending insurance, usually from morn until late evening, regrettably missing most family dinners. Harold enjoyed few avocations except playing the guitar or banjo and listening to sports on the radio, both of which faded some in his later years. Although I hasten to add that our Father was scheduled to play a New Year's Eve gig, with his Lion's Club band, the very week after he died on Christmas Eve, 1987.

We talk about today's kids being robbed of their childhoods by parents thrusting them into nonstop, frenetic activity. Such is clearly a major social crisis. However, could it also be true that our society is robbing seniors of a satisfying elderhood, which requires an abundance of tranquility and renewal ... of inner liberty?

Harold Towle couldn't sit still, tolerate silence, and yield to being, just being. He was productive in his own fashion, but hardly fulfilled as a man. He deserved better. My Dad got *older* without becoming much of an *elder*. His heart and spirit grew dim; then his body crumbled. He kept trudging into the office, continuing to sell insurance and then a few months shy of 82 years of age, Harold Towle was wearing out, so he came home; mainly, I think, to arrange financial matters for his precious Mary's future. We still have Dad's scrawled notes and numbers to confirm that mission! Within a matter of a few weeks, he got ill, went to the hospital, and died behind a closed door.

I love my father dearly, and rarely a day passes that I don't think of him, mostly when crooning the songs we cherished in common. And both of his boys went into "helping" professions, emulating our father who considered himself a "counselor" more than a salesman. Furthermore, I can't really quarrel with his manner of shutting down and ambling off alone, as animals often do in the woods, for he knew no other way. But it won't be mine.

As long as my legs allow, now at 83 (both my brother, at 86, and I have outlived our father), I've awakened to the physical and spiritual benefits of walking, using native easterner Henry David Thoreau (1817-1862), life-long abolitionist *and* naturalist, as my guide.

Thoreau claimed that "it is a great art to saunter," and so it is. Sauntering poses the optimal Sabbath activity, still moving but in unrushed fashion. The saunterer is one who strolls in measured manner, with one eye on nature, the other on soul, treating the land, and all therein, as holy. The saunterer is on a quest—not for exercise so much as for exploration, less for recreation and more for re-creation. It's not the length but the depth of walk that makes it sacrosanct.

Sauntering was not extraneous but indispensable to Thoreau's daily fare. He would walk in the woods up to four hours each day and scoffed at those who considered sauntering worthless.

Although occasionally Thoreau would have walking companions, he normally walked alone. He put it bluntly: "Ask me for a certain number of dollars if you will, but do not ask me for my afternoons." Do you as a young adult, mid-lifer, or senior, ramble a bit every day, exploring the nooks and crannies of your city or countryside? And do you prefer to saunter alone or accompanied?

Saunterers stride in reverent, appreciative gait, treading upon the land, every piece of it, as hallowed, touching the earth with deft hands and tender feet (there was nothing between Thoreau's soles and the soil except the skin of an animal). Saunterers awake, as is the Hindu custom, to caress the earth each morn, strike it gently, and then apologize for trampling upon it in the hours ahead.

A second, albeit unusual, source of Sabbath for me is weeping. The Christian Beatitude notes: "Blessed are they who mourn, for they shall be comforted." Little mourning, little comfort. Sufi poet and chanter Doug von Koss has vowed that whenever the flow of tears comes, he will let them wet his cheeks, then tumble, unwiped, to the ground. For when our tears moisten the earth, they invariably supplement the soil and sprout something.

There's copious biblical support for crying. Near the end of that chaotic tale of intrigue, betrayal, and forgiveness between Joseph and his brothers, Joseph is so overcome with emotion (particularly feelings of fondness for his kin) that he dissolves in tears. Joseph weeps, not once, twice, or three times, but on six different occasions.

In the Christian Scriptures, it's reported: "And Jesus wept." This may be the shortest verse in the entire bible, but what a mighty phrase! Jesus was distraught over the rotten behavior of his own people, and instead of ranting and railing, instead of drafting an oration, instead of assembling forces to mount a political response, he was moved to tears. Sometimes falling to pieces is the only way to put ourselves back together again.

I know that the older I get, the weepier I am, unapologetically so. I've experienced so much joy and sadness in my eight plus decades that my moans and groans can often only cascade in tears. In the Talmudic tradition, one places several tear-cups on the mantel, and at the end of the day, you march forthwith to the mantel, step high on your tiptoes, and deposit an entire day's worth of tears into the assorted cups of angst and anger, aloneness and anguish, as well as other designated containers of gladness and gratitude and hope positioned upon the shelf jutting from your fireplace. The measure of one's soulfulness is gauged by the abundance of water filling those tear-cups.

Americans, especially men, are notorious for trying to tough things out. Our masculinity problem is too little weeping for our own good, let alone the good of others. The cost is often great, as one physician aptly states: "Sorrows that find no vent in tears may soon make other organs weep." We cry because we're feeling animals. The wetter ... the better.

Too many of us hanker to bypass pain and race unscathed toward the land of bliss. However, without experiencing a healthy dosage of discomfort, our lives deliver erratic pleasure and minimal solace. Relief, yea, moments of restorative Sabbath, come to those who grieve openly and ongoingly.

One evening, Buddha heard wailing in a house he was passing and, upon entering inconspicuously, he found that the householder had died, and the family and neighbors were weeping. Immediately, Buddha sat down and began crying too. An elderly gentleman, shaken by this show of distress in such an illustrious guru, kvetched: "I would have thought that you, the Buddha, were beyond such emotional outbursts!" "On the contrary, it's precisely this crying that helps me through life," Buddha replied, sobbing away.

Now, onward to my principal source of Sabbath fuel, singing:

I will sing unto the Lord as long as I live.
—Psalm 104:33

*Singing is inner massage; put your hand
on your chest and you'll know what I mean!*
—Judy Fjell

For me, singing surpasses being either an art or a science in any conventional sense. Singing qualifies more as a spirited venture that evokes merriment and meaning from both the known and the furtive recesses of one's being. When warbling, my spirit can neither frown nor flounder. Singing bathes me in radiance; then it rouses me to deliver mercy and love throughout the course of my day.

Whether you sing in an organized choir, perform instrumentally in a community orchestra, or coyly hum melodies in a private corner of your house, if music-making lifts your soul, it qualifies as a bona fide spiritual practice. Your sense of rhythm, melody, or harmony may be limited, and the sounds that emanate from your throat may not always be euphonious, yet singing still stirs your very being. If that's the case, you're blessed by an oft-ignored and undervalued source of sabbathing right inside the temple of your body.

One's larynx comes with birth. Every one of us possesses our own encased instrument, to be employed at beck and call. The human voice box isn't cumbersome to lug about like a saxophone and cello or doesn't have to be borrowed like a friend's piano. Singing is physically accessible and financially reasonable. Eminently portable, we can sing wherever and whenever: whether gathered around a campfire or taking a shower, during a sermon or at a social justice rally. Few locations are off-bounds to warble forth one's interior.

Another benefit of singing is its astonishing dexterity, being one of those rare activities geared for either private or public enjoyment. I personally possess a sacred corner of our attic or *Meryloft* (a word that combines the names of our deceased mother Marys with the art of Merrymaking) where I hole up to sing every genre of music from spirituals to folk, country western to rock, pop to semi-classical melodies ... sometimes *a capella*, other times accompanied by my guitar. And when I'm alone, more often than not, I find myself humming, whistling, chanting, or singing softly or loudly, slowly or swiftly.

A supplemental reward of singing is how it's linked me with cherished family members. My father was a consummate musician, but I never learned musical skills directly from him. Ah, such is often the parent-child quandary, right? However, now that he's dead, every time I pick up the 1947 Gibson guitar Dad bequeathed me and croon a melody, Harold Alexander Towle's spirit vibrates through my voice.

And during her waning years, the only thing that would seemingly calm my cherished mother-in-law's agitated soul was my singing melodies of her era and mine. As she suffered from the cognitive decline of tiny strokes, singing seemed to ground Mary's soul and brought a sparkle to her countenance. Isn't it miraculous how singing insinuates its way, beneath all words, into our deepest crux?

On the other end of our generational sweep, there was nothing (they're in their twenties now), that connected me more deeply with our young grandchildren than holding them on my lap while navigating love-songs and lullabies. Intimacy was bred from such smells, sights, and sounds. Unforgettable.

And when Carolyn and I sing together, we assuredly replenish the wellsprings of our priceless love. We "found" one another through singing; we continued to "grow" one another through singing. And I sang to her as she was dying.

In my view, authentic joy should furnish sufficient nutrients for all the regions of the self. And singing does just that. As Paul wrote in I Corinthians 14:15: "I will sing with the spirit, and I will sing with the mind also." That's certainly the balance I seek when choosing tunes that awaken my spirit as well as stretch my mind. But that's not all. Singing is an endeavor that occupies one's body. As contemporary folk-singer Holly Near (1949-) pens in her autobiography, *Fire in the Rain, Singer in the Storm*:

> *If I were to point at my voice, I would not be pointing at my throat but rather at my eyes and cheeks and lips and jaw and shoulders and chest and arms and trunk and thighs and feet. This morning I sang a note. I could hear my heartbeat in the note.*

You see, when we sing, not only do our vocal chords tremble, but some of our bones rattle. Singing exudes raw physicality, enthralling both our heartbeat and our breath. It's an in-body, full-body experience.

Singing spurs the development of our conscience as well, for there's never been a social movement that hasn't been soaked in song. Justice-building is yoked with joy-sharing. Furthermore, singing triggers heart-growth, enabling us to find a heartened voice in a dreary, oft-heartless world.

Singing also connects my physically-hobbled and cognitively-challenged cohorts in nursing homes more closely with the present world. Despite acute infirmities and feelings of futility, when residents at PACE, Balboa Convalescent, or Harbor View join me in song, most everyone in the room feels more animated. Memories are kindled and moods bolstered.

Just the other day, we were collectively brooding over the religious, ethnic, environmental, and racial strife engulfing our globe … everywhere from the Gaza Strip to natural disasters to our local San Diego neighborhoods. Our spirits were drooping, so I kept turning to songs that might elevate our disposition such as *"I'm On My Way," "Stand By Me," "This Little Light of Mine," "Hava Nagila," "Lean on Me," "We are the World,"* and *"What a Wonderful World,"* which, by the way, was written as an antidote to the racially-charged climate of the United States in the 1960's. Despite the torrent of violence sweeping our contemporary society, Louis Armstrong's song of yesteryear still reminds us, young and old alike, that it can be "a wonderful world," if you and I dare to contribute our fair share to make it so. So, every time I hoist my guitar to play, I resonate with the words engraved upon the circumference of premier American folk singer and activist, Pete Seeger's (1919-2014) banjo: "This instrument surrounds hate with love and forces it to surrender!"

My songs are generally chosen according to the following criteria: (1) simple and sing-able; (2) familiar to most elders and crones;

although now that I sing at the Homeless Center, I've broadened my selections; (3) songs with a positive, reassuring message such as *Everything is Beautiful, He/She/They Ain't Heavy, Amazing Grace,* and *That's What Friends are For.*

And, of course, there are plenty of frisky tunes such as *Mairzy Doats* and comfort songs such as *Swing Low, Sweet Chariot.* I sometimes even change the lyrics to furnish a more inclusive message. I remember once adding, during the second verse of *America the Beautiful,* "sisterhood," to the traditional "brotherhood," and one woman's eyes beamed with glee.

We also croon love ballads such as *You are My Sunshine, Always, Side by Side,* and *Fly Me to the Moon,* because most everyone in nursing homes can readily identify with romance—past, present, or future. Recently, a new resident, David, has taken quite a fancy to Rose, even holding her hand, in-between bites of food. Usually sullen, Rose's face is now aglow, so clearly we're never too old for ample forms of *amor*. Consequently, you'll hear me serenading these two love-birds, from time to time, with a passionate version of *The Rose.*

Some of the nursing home participants even rock and reel along the way. My lead dancer at PACE (*Programs of All-inclusive Care for the Elderly*) is Michael who, although suffering from cognitive decline, will rise from his seat when moved by a particular song. While on his feet, Michael sways back and forth to the rhythm, occasionally nodding to one of the caregivers or other clients to join him in dancing. Last week, Michael lured Mengistu, another regular, into a fetching escapade of two men tangoing. Now, just about every week, the "M Brothers" gambol to their heart's content and the room's delight.

There was also a memorable moment when I sang *God Bless America*. Periodically, I'll relate some of the background of certain songs. I try not to overdo it, since people want music more than chatter; but, in this instance, I recalled how Irving Berlin (1888-1989) wrote *God Bless America* while serving in the American military in World War I. Berlin filed the song away, deeming it a bit too chauvinistic to release, since he was a recent Jewish immigrant from Siberia and hadn't yet earned his patriotic stripes. Then, when World War II rolls around, singer Kate Smith (1907-1986) learns about *God Bless America*, and wonders where in the world this exquisite ballad has been hidden all those intervening decades. Smith proceeded to make it famous, indeed, perhaps America's favorite national anthem. But when the Ku Klux Klan (the violent, white supremacist society founded in 1915) learned that it was written by a Jewish émigré, they vehemently protested, levelling a bigoted attack on Berlin.

A woman in the nursing home, whose back always faced me when she was eating, intrepidly turned around, after I had finished singing *God Bless America*, and blurted out, with tears in her eyes: "Tom, those people are my people, and that story of prejudice resembles my own story! Please, let's belt it out again, this time as a prayer for a better America." I never sing *God Bless America* without thinking about Ida Bloomberg, now of blessed memory.

Not all is sweetness and light, since some of my buddies in nursing homes occasionally call me to account. Delores loves my music and spends as much time humming and singing as she does enjoying her lunch. By the way, I remind the residents that there's both physical *and* soul food. Since both are crucial for life's homestretch, I encourage folks to eat up, listen up, and sing up! Well,

Delores, of Hispanic lineage—as are 50% of the residents and 80% of the caregivers—recently rose from her chair, a rare occurrence, since she's wheelchair bound, and said in a barbed voice; "Hey, amigo, is *De Colores* the only Spanish song you know?" And I had to confess that it was, but then I rallied to respond: "Okay, Delores, let's see if I'm not too old to be bold!"

Two months later, after *mucho* grinding, I returned to Balboa nursing home with new Spanish ballads that I've been rotating into my repertoire such as *La Bamba, Cuando Caliente el Sol, Guantanamera, Eres Tu,* and *Dime*.

Disappointingly, I've never internalized much of my own mixed Mexican ancestry, except for this modest, late-life singing sortie. Plus my Spanish stinks; but it matters not, because Delores and others now feel more included when the visiting "gringo" croons ballads from "their" esteemed heritage.

Not all my singing gigs are successful, believe me. There've been times when my voice is hoarse or cracking, times when my waist-band amplifier dies on the spot, and times when I'm bushed or everyone else in the room would rather be doing anything but listening to my chirruping. Once, I grew intrigued by a new guy in the back of the PACE cafeteria, who happened to be rocking back and forth. He seemed to be grooving to my tunes, but upon closer observation, I realized that he had a headset on and was chilling to his own music. And, of course, like any "bar scene," there are folks blithely gabbing or munching away in the background. And so it goes!

And my moments of Sabbath discipline are incomplete without *chanting*, singing's proverbial cousin. If the song is linear, the chant is circular. A chant takes a basic truth and anchors it spiritually through repetition. Chants are so versatile. We can share them while walking, driving a car (however, only if stalled in traffic), or residing quietly in our office. They can be learned in a matter of minutes and furnish a mantra for one's daily scramble. I enjoy chants from various traditions: Jewish, Christian, Hindu, Sufi, Buddhist, and Native American. Oh, I could go on musing about music as a fundamental source of my personal Sabbath sustenance, but enough is enough.

Suffice it to say, when I come to die, if I'm lucky enough, after I've uttered some good-byes and shared tears with my beloveds, I'd like to be alone, and as my voice is willing, sing some sort of thank you to God for a hallowed journey beyond my wildest dreams. I hardly know what special melody or medley I'll choose to sing, since there's so much music crowding my spirit. I beam at the prospect of being able to go out singing.

I now want to salute two additional pilgrims who honored and kept the Sabbath via finding solace in nature.

First, Elijah. The days that follow Elijah's triumph over hundreds of Baal priests are depressing ones. The public cheering quickly leaves Elijah and turns to follow his enemy, Queen Jezebel. Elijah feels deserted by Yahweh as well. Despondent and anxious, Elijah headed into the wilderness. He was willing to die: "It is enough, now, take away my life; for I am no better than my fathers."

Then Elijah flees to a cave and lodges there. Grousing in defeatism, Elijah hears the various sounds of earthquake, wind, and fire, but God's voice dwells in none of these loud, even violent, upheavals. He suddenly hears a "still, small voice" imploring him, "What are you doing here, Elijah?" Note this "quiet, subdued voice" (another translation) is strikingly unlike the booming, even forbidding, voice of God in the movie *Ten Commandments*!

In other words, what's your purpose in life now? What remains on your spiritual itinerary, Elijah? He balks; then Yahweh probes a second time, more strongly, following this question with a command for Elijah to return home, anoint another religious leader to take his place, then retire and rest in peace ... which is what came to pass.

Elijah went to the woods to hide away from God and humanity, collect his thoughts, and nurse his wounds. God's piercing call reached the prophet through the "sound of a gentle stillness," a sound both baffling and energizing, yet insistently real. Elijah finally found Sabbath.

Most of us, when pressed, need to learn and practice, the "slowdown" arts: like brooding or sitting pensively; dawdling or loitering without purpose; and hovering or fluttering about, suspended in the air. Hushing and power-lounging also deliver moments of Sabbath. As the Jewish writer of yore, Ecclesiastes, put it (4:6): "Better is one handful of quietness than two hands full of toil and a striving after wind."

Talking *per se* is of no particular value. "A word spoken in due season," as Proverbs suggests, is what truly counts: the right word at the right time in the right place. As they say, the health of any vital love bond or friendship is often measured by the number of teeth marks in our tongue. There's an unwritten law in Vermont that people are not to speak unless they are certain that what they have to say will be an improvement upon the silence. That's the rule of Quaker worship, too.

We adults yearn to learn how to "turn up the quiet" as we age. We hanker to be still and acknowledge that we don't truly own everything, even our souls; we merely inhabit them. We wish to be still and permit hidden, unconscious streams to flow. We seek to be still and invite the fountain of tears to pour forth. We long to be still and allow clarity to come to the muddy pool of our confused spirits. I say *allow*, because we can never produce, garner, or win the grace of being still. We can only invite or stifle its presence. We thirst to hold *and* keep the Sabbath, not just weekly but daily, every one of us.

A second biblical exemplar of sabbathing: Jesus. Great interest surrounded the start of the Nazarene's ministry—40 days in the wilderness, and at its close—a lonely vigil in the garden—but we forget that the Jewish prophet took micro-breaks, all his days and nights. The Christian scriptures recount Jesus withdrawing from life's tumult on a regular basis: "And when he had sent the multitude away, Jesus went up into a mountain apart to pray; and when the evening was come, he was there alone." (Matthew 14:23)

In Christian folklore, some folks reportedly came to Jesus and wanted to know what they must *do* to inherit the realm of God (Mark 5:36 and 10:21). Much to their amazement and consternation, the Rabbi responded that it would not take doing but *being* something. Not surprisingly, most inquirers turned aside and trudged off. You and I need to find our mountains and wellsprings where we can go "apart to pray" or simply sit, replenishing our souls.

There was something hauntingly reserved about Jesus. As the spiritual goes, "Jesus walked this lonesome valley; he had to walk it by himself ..." But, in the final round, that same gospel hymn notes that all human beings have to walk through life's lonesome valley, at one time or another. Hence, the optimal way to fulfill our true selves, whether we're 20 or 40 or 80 or 100, is to spend abundant moments, in rhythmic measure, both alone and together.

Being solitary and solidary requires an exchange of one letter, but both are soulful necessities. I don't know about you, but I refuse to go to my grave without a more intimate knowledge of who I am—this maddeningly obstinate yet resourceful creature whose skin I've been inhabiting all my existence—me, myself, and I ... truly, my first and final friend.

Honoring the Sabbath is a visible reminder that every one of us is more than a cog in the economic, social, or familial machine, that we have a divine right to rest and restore our very bodies and minds. Sabbath is the sacred time when we declare a truce from all our weekly wrangling and bring our personal universe to some semblance of serenity. Have you noticed that when we dare to observe quality moments of Sabbath, the other nine commandments seem more manageable?

Gunilla Norris, meditation teacher and psychotherapist, deftly phrases the sustenance found in Sabbath:

> *These little steps bring something of our selves back to the whole, the way a bee brings nectar to its hive ... the pauses add up.*

For religious folk like Jews and Christians, Hindus and Moslems, Buddhists and Taoists, the Sabbath is not only a day denoting the absence of work; it's far more. Sabbath heralds a way of traversing space and time that includes outbreaks of song and delight, naps and rituals, rumination and banter. I contribute weekly as a "singing companion" in nursing homes as well as in the courtyard at the Homeless Center, and I progressively realize that gaps are sacred both in music and life. Yes, the pauses add up.

In the summer of 2023, Carolyn and I sought a revitalizing sabbath in our marriage. We chose to celebrate our 50th anniversary navigating a supremely peaceful time in Tahiti. We went to French Polynesia not for snorkeling, diving, or hiking but solely for soaking in the sunshine and quietude of this beautiful land. We pursued a spiritual breather to restore our bodies and enrich our partnership. And we decided fortuitously to go a few months before our actual celebration on November 16th—blessedly, because Carolyn died on October 23rd.

We took a week-long Paul Gauguin Cruise into remote harbors on the Society Islands, bursting with picturesque landscapes, sublime lagoons, and lush rainforests. It furnished an opportunity to cherish the manifold roots and branches of our ever-evolving love. We sought sensual connection and abundant smiles. We slowed down. We sabbathed.

Legendary, post-Impressionist French painter, Paul Gauguin (1848-1903) had moved from Paris to the South Pacific in 1891 hoping to find an Arcadian realm of "ecstasy, peace and art ... where living means singing and loving." Carolyn's father, Millard Sheets (1907-1989), also found Tahiti (especially Moorea) to be an idyllic setting for one of his world-wide, painting workshops.

Our celebratory trek proved fruitful as well. We returned to Southern California, pacified of mind and body ... our marriage invigorated for the *daze* ahead. After all, partnership, at its richest, is for marathoners not sprinters. I appreciate the way Spanish diplomat and writer, Salvador de Madraiga (1886-1978) put it: "Love me little by little, be not in haste. For I would have you love me long. Love me slowly, love me deeply, love me long."

Our loving bonds need to be reminded constantly of the importance of *slowth*. There's an apt poster in a marriage therapist's office which shows a cuddly puppy, head tilted at an angle with a wistful look, that reads: "I don't need a great deal of love, but I do need a steady supply." We partners don't hanker for sporadic, mega-doses of tenderness but thirst for daily signs of affection. Tokens of endearment ... calmly delivered.

We need to grasp our beloved's hand, without a word, before we tackle a scary engagement or meeting. We need our mate to say "thank you" for something we've done a thousand times. We need to express abrasive news in a velvety manner. We need casual walks and ponderous talks. We need to respect our partner's opinions even when we find them weird or burdensome. We need full-body love with hands and lips leisurely caressing one another from head to toes. Yes, we need a steady supply of love.

Every time I mount the pulpit nowadays, either via zoom across the land or somewhere in my home region, I launch my sermons by crooning a patch of Kate Wolf's ballad: *Give Yourself to Love*, composed in 1982, shortly before she prematurely died of leukemia, at the age of 44. It's a particularly poignant song in my repertoire and grounds my soul before I grapple with moral or spiritual subject matter.

> *You must give yourself to love,*
> *if love is what you're after.*
> *Open up your hearts to*
> *the tears and laughter,*
> *and give yourself to love,*
> *give yourself to love.*

That mellow refrain spurs me to deliver my sermon awash in tenderness, while reminding listeners (whatever the specific theme of the morning worship service might be!) that love is truly the vitalizing principle of all our days and nights.

And Wolf's final verse serves as a wake-up call, lest our love give way to schmaltz:

Love is born in fire; it's planted like a seed.
And love can't give you everything,
but it gives you what you need.
And love comes when you're ready,
love comes when you're afraid,
it will be your greatest teacher;
the best friend you have made.

I could parse each phrase in that powerful stanza, but I'll leave that to you. Take a few moments now and explicate Wolf's wisdom for the affectionate bonds of your own voyage.

One more angle on love, marital love ... my own. After returning from Tahiti, Carolyn kept stressing something fresh regarding our marriage. She'd insightfully quip: "Tom, you know what? We're ultimately all we have. Our love is it!" Initially, I hastened to amend her sentiment with: "Yes, that's true, but what about our family's bountiful love for each of us. And what about our dear friends; we can't minimize their conveyed affection and respect!"

But wisely, I shut up, and bathed in her heartfelt gratitude and fondness. She was discerning that when push came to shove, when bleakness crept into our days and nights, when no one else was around ... we *were* it. Our marital love was primal and core, unlike any other love we've been blessed to enjoy! Carolyn was spot on. Our love, albeit imperfect, "gave us what we needed." And always would. We could keep returning to one another's steadfast embrace, all the way to one of our graves, and then our embrace would manifest soulfully.

Back to the pertinence and power of Sabbath. The scriptures remind us that the Sabbath is given to us and created for us, not the other way around. That's a handy reminder, for Sabbath-time loses its pertinence and power, if it becomes another batch of compulsions, untrue to one's heart. Rather the Sabbath summons us to find our own optimal ways to smile, relax, and breathe.

Just breathe. Breathing is an activity destined for self-nourishment, to be sure, but it also constitutes our main link with all existence. For the same air flows in and out of the lungs of all living things. The regular practice of conscious breathing has proven to reduce stress, blood pressure, and cholesterol levels. Furthermore, breathing is an essential and core part of meditation. A Harvard study discovered that nursing home patients, who were in their eighties when they first began meditation, felt more cheerful, on the whole functioned better, even lived longer than non-meditators.

I remain an unpolished meditator but have become a lively, spur-of-the moment chanter as well as a daily reciter of soothing mantras such as that of Vietnamese Buddhist monk, Thich Nhat Hanh (1926-2022): "Breathing in, I calm my body and mind. Breathing out, I smile. Dwelling in the present moment, I know that this is the only moment." Then I aspire to spend the rest of my day observing said wisdom. How do you, dear siblings, soothe and stabilize your spirit?

The testimony of those who have meditated in the Hindu, Buddhist, and Sufi traditions, as well as Jewish and Christian mysticism, is that breathing is at once, ordinary and transcendent. To breathe deeply is a religious act, wherein our individual spirit partakes of the Infinite Spirit.

Myriad humans have prayed and chanted, danced and sung, studied and meditated, perhaps visited a sacred site or been on a holy pilgrimage, but often during the afternoon of life, we come to the realization that there's nothing nearer the hub of spiritual contentment than paying close attention to our own breathing in and breathing out.

Having every one of the 75 trillion cells in our bodies breathing more slowly and harmoniously is decisive to a hale and holy existence.

> ### Study questions for personal reflection and/or group discussion

(1) How and when do you inhale and exhale daily in intentional fashion?

(2) Remember Sabbath entails resting with respect to time *and* space. Address both.

(3) In what ways do you intentionally *saunter* daily?

(4) Does crying, singing, or meditation play any restorative role in your life?

(5) As you age, do you find yourself drawn increasingly to the power of *slowth*? If so, name the ways?

(6) How do you intentionally nourish and renew your primary bonds of love and friendship?

(7) Can you identify with the life-rhythms of either Elijah or Jesus?

(8) Put into words, however inadequately, the role and place of *breathing* in your existence.

Chapter V

Value Your Primal Bond

V. Honor your father and your mother, that your days may be long in the land which the Lord your God gives you.
—Exodus 20:12

The great events of this world are not battles and elections and earthquakes and thunderbolts. The great events are babies, for each child comes with the message that God is not yet discouraged with humanity but is still expecting goodwill to become incarnate in each human life. And so God produced each of us to guide the Earth toward peace rather than conflict.
—Marian Wright Edelman

Making the decision to have a child is momentous. It is to decide, forever, to have your heart go walking around outside your body.
—Elizabeth Stone

All parents, for better or worse, shape our lives. The imprint is unavoidable. It marks us into old age.
—Chris Hedges

Family solidarity was as crucial for the Hebrews as breathing and eating. In the Akan language in Ghana, the word *sankofa* means to look forward by looking back, literally, "to reach back and get it or go back and fetch it." All of *it*: the good, the bad, and the average. We cherish the past even as we chart the future. We fully open our hearts, in Taoist fashion, to "ten thousand joys and ten thousand sorrows!" Such is the holistic approach to honoring our family heritage.

However, the word *honor* reminds us not to romanticize our parents but rather to take them seriously, the only way parents ought to be taken. The parent-child nexus, being our first and most enduring human bond, provides the lodestar of all relationships. We learn how to express or suppress affection and respectfulness, beginning in the home.

Some of us suffered what's called the "crime of a happy childhood." I entered this world ardently wanted by parents who were in their 30's. Hence, I've always believed, even in the gloomiest of hours, that I possessed ontological "okayness" and that it was good I was alive. While negotiating life's shocks as well as travesties of my own doing, I've been upheld by a replenishable pool of love. I've felt cradled in the bosom of fondness, both human and divine, from the get-go. I received the motherly caress, not perfectly, but amply nourishing for my journey. I resonate with the mindset of Helen Dunmore's benedictory poem:

> *Death, hold out your arms for me.*
> *Embrace me, give me your motherly caress.*

Nevertheless, the parent-child bond is an oft-tense, even throbbing, struggle, and it plays out in unexpected ways. Countless children have been neglected or abused by their parents, so love may not be possible in these cases. But honor is manageable, because it recognizes the vital function of being a parent. At its core, the vocation of parenting needs to be held in high regard, so that children, (even if harmed as a youngster) might become honorable parents themselves someday. However, before we can fully honor our parents as individuals, we will often need to enact forgiveness, in both directions.

Another spin on #5: if your parents fall short of the honoring standard, then broaden this commandment to esteem other adults who nurture your development. The surrogate parent could be a neighbor, teacher, or gardener. As singer and civil rights activist Harry Belafonte (1927-2023) prudently remarked: "Today's children can't find enough adults!" The parenting adventure is strife-ridden, and all available adults are necessary, at some moment, to show up and support a child who might need strength and savvy. Sometimes, another grown-up proves to be a supplemental, or even more fitting, parent to us than our own *given* ones. It's what one psychologist has appropriately labeled "*alloparenting!*"

The Hebrew scriptures invite us to *honor* parents in this commandment, while, nearby in another book, it urges us to *leave* them: namely, at the point when we children forge our own adult lives and bonds, posing one of life's bristliest yet most essential relational passages. Honor our folks, then dare to separate from them, making sufficient peace with the parent-child link, all the way to our respective graves.

As an adult who has been a bio, adoptive, and step father, I've found it to be the most challenging of all my professions, ranging from personhood to ministry. The word "honor" in Hebrew is *kabod* which signifies "glory" or "weight."

Unquestionably, parenting has been both a glorious *and* a weighty occupation for me. As they say, having a child in the house is like living with a Zen master: it requires constant attention, patience, elasticity, sacrifice, and selflessness. Surely, many readers will identify with this characterization.

Colleague Meg Barnhouse phrases it poignantly:

> *To a new parent, our child will make mistakes, as they grow and some of those will make you cry. Being a parent is not for the faint of heart. Try to be in control of yourself rather than your child, and you'll be okay. Love is hard on the heart. Your heart can't remain perfect and proud, unscarred and perky. It will be worn and joyous, wise and beat up and full of sorrow and amazement.*

Predictably, we often fall short as both parent and child. Austrian-born American child psychologist Bruno Bettelheim (1903-1990), who had a checkered career himself as a father, wrote: "There are no perfect parents and no perfect children, but every parent can be good enough." And I would add: every child can be good enough as well!

Here's a laundry list of some of the lessons I've garnered in my decades of parenting, grand-parenting, and now great-grand-parenting.

First, parenting isn't for everyone. Blessedly, today's parenthood is becoming more of an intentional choice than the expectation of my generation. Some adults don't feel particularly comfortable around children. Others enjoy children but don't need their own; they already have access to a whole caboodle of youngers around:

nieces and nephews, neighbors and students. Parenting is merely one way to shape society and definitely needs to be a chosen rather than a pressured or presumed path. No one is a better human being, just because they're breeders or adopters.

Second, parenting requires a village. Think of parenting in this way, framed by one of my own mentors: a good home provides the protection of sturdy walls and a sheltering roof, but windows and doors are also essential. Through windows our children glimpse a larger world and through doors come friends and strangers into their lives, full of instruction, sometimes good and sometimes bad, but not appreciably distinct from the mixtures we parents dispense.

Third, parents need to practice what the Buddhists call "creative detachment." Or as Sydney Harris (1917-1986), American journalist, implores: "Remember that children are people, not parental ornaments." We parents are related to all of our kids, but we aren't ultimately responsible for any of them. Some parents mistakenly grab the lion's share of credit or blame for how our children turn out without allowing them to shoulder the greater part themselves. Incontestably, we play a critical role in their formation, but they develop their own singular identities.

The parental desire to re-create one's self through one's child poses a demoralizing blind spot as well as a policy doomed to failure. That's why during children celebrations, I often recite Lebanese-American poet, Kahlil Gibran's (1883-1931) declaration of independence:

> *Your children are not your children. They come through you but not from you, and though they are with you, they belong not to you ... You may give them your love but not your thoughts, for they have their own thoughts.*

We aren't the eventual determiners of our children's destinies; they are. We have children on loan, for a while, perhaps 20% or so of their entire lives, bunking at our abode and benefitting from our resources, our counsel, and our gaffes. Then willingly or reluctantly, we release them to the wider world for their own blossoming. Children need the persistent and life-long support of parents in the quest for personal agency. Individuation is their supreme goal.

What it comes down to is parents being "adult" enough to proclaim the following: "We have created and cradled a life; now let the child have it. Let her/him/them decide what they want to be and do with their own existence." Our children have inalienable rights to become what they're capable and desirous of becoming, no matter how dissimilar from us or our "virtuous" blueprints their choices might pan out. Mature parenting does not judge, pressure, over-expect, or control children. Love finally accepts their preferences and evolution. Nine words have tried to steer my parenting course: "whenever possible, remain available for them ... here and now!"

Fourth, parents love their children differently. When we don't, we either fail to admit it or pummel ourselves in the woodshed. We usually (not always) love all our children and invariably from beginning to end. But love isn't enough. Gratifying parenthood also demands some "liking" of our children, and that can vary markedly from child unto child. Whereas we take for granted that adults mesh with some adults and wrangle, even flounder, with others, we somehow expect equal levels of enjoyment with respect to our parent-child bonds. The fact is that certain children are, on the whole, more pleasurable than others due to personality resemblance or relational rhythm or whatever. Some parents and children just go together well, and others don't; we parents need to make adequate peace with that reality.

Comparisons are odious, and I don't recommend blatantly telling certain of our children that we enjoy them more or less than the others, although it's seldom a secret to anybody in the family, right? Yet it's liberating for parents to know that we aren't lousy parent-people, just because we love our children differently and enjoy them unequally. And, of course, the same goes for children's attitudes toward and treatment of their respective parents.

Fifth, parent-child bonds aren't always successful.

The ultimate test of even the most enlightened guru is to go home and spend a healthy weekend with their parents!
—RAM DASS

As long as we're swimming the murky, doleful waters of parenting, let's travel one fathom deeper. Most manuals announce that in parent-child conflicts, everyone can win, and, furthermore, that resentments will eventually melt away. That's certainly our prayerful hope and often can transpire, but let's not wax unduly romantic.

In the Egyptian Coptic version of the Christian Scriptures, there's a disturbing passage where Jesus declares that "no one can enter the realm of heaven until they have dealt both with their love and hate toward their parents."

Wow, that's mighty stern counsel coming from one of the masterful peace-makers of history. Nonetheless, it furnishes spiritual wisdom, since myriad sons, daughters, and *trans* children remain emotionally clogged, because they aren't permitted to voice and vent their sincerely felt ambivalent emotions toward their parents.

Given the right conditions, counseling, timing, and lots of good karma, healing can occur. Hence, no parent-child relationship can ever be utterly kicked to the curb. Memories of affection and possibilities for hope endure, and they should. I personally heed the Hindu wisdom in all of my interpersonal bonds, namely: "Don't ever throw anyone out of your heart!" Faith, hope, and love have certainly sustained our family through some dismal and disastrous days and propelled us toward moments of mending. Even, here and now, as my pen scrawls these very words.

But, and here's a major *but*: we humans live with profound sorrows and irreconcilable breaks everywhere in our existence, both outside and inside our families. As they say, if we can feel it, we can heal it. However, sometimes we obstruct our feelings, and any viable road toward relational mending is blocked. The painful verity is that sometimes parents are impelled to divorce their own children *and* vice versa. Then, to scapegoat or second guess either ourselves or our children merely aggravates the anguish. Not all parent-child bonds have happy beginnings, middles, or endings.

Sixth, adults parent primarily according to their own needs.

I have a cartoon that shows a father holding his child over his knee and spanking him. It reads: "First, I'd like to destroy a ridiculous myth … this isn't going to hurt me more than it hurts you!" Now, I neither believe in corporal punishment nor did I ever practice it with our offspring. Yet there's a deeper myth at work here, a pervasive one in our parenting culture. The myth says: "I'm doing this for your own good, for your own benefit, my child!" Let's come clean and clear about why we parents usually do something. The reality is that you and I parent primarily according to what we perceive to be good for ourselves as fathers and mothers. How could we do otherwise? It's presumptuous to claim full knowledge of what's good for our children, especially when they mature to decision-making age.

Check it out: so much of what we say our children need is actually either what we want or need them to get or what we want or need to give. A mundane example: if I want a hug from one of my children, then I need to go after it rather than beg or barter for it. This is my guideline: "give and ye shall often receive, wait to receive and ye shall usually resent." Undoubtedly, it's a delight when our children respond naturally to our gestures and gifts of love. It's a thrill when they reciprocate and initiate too. But their responses can't be predicted, promised, or programmed. Plus, our children don't owe us anything. We brought them into our hearth and heart. Anything they deliver in response is a bonus. Therefore, the honoring invited in this 5th commandment is truly a gift.

There are no guarantees in life as in parenting—only opportunities. So, I've learned to seize them. I've tried to beat my children to the draw, to give them some undivided attention as frequently as I could before they stood up and clamored for it. Not for their sake so much as for my own. And all too soon, we learn, don't we, that we parents covet the presence of our children more than they need ours ... as they age out of our clutches.

We've taken each of our grandchildren on a mutually determined week-long expedition to some colorful, exciting place such as Costa Rica, Alaska, New York, and the Canyonlands of the Southwest. We've done so when they're ten-years-old, because we've found that, at that age, they're still interested in holding our hands, playing games with us, and even sleeping in the same bed.

When they've reached teenage-hood, they may still love us, but they're appropriately no longer "into" us. They're "separating," and gravitating toward their peers, and texting on their cell-phones. That's just the way growing up unfurls.

Seventh, parents don't raise children. The widespread notion is that the parents' job is to raise their children to be happy and responsible humans. I second the responsible part but eschew both the happy and the raise part. My friend sensibly remarked to her 15-year-old son: "By the way, Malcolm, in case you've forgotten; you're not always going to be happy. So, I urge you to get used to disappointment and frustration. I want you, in good and bad times, to go to Malcolm, to keep becoming the best version of yourself possible." That's the healthy and responsible thing to do.

And, furthermore, we may raise flags, funds, blinds, arms, and corn, but we don't raise other human beings. Of course, we prepare an environment, and we educate ourselves as parents, but children systematically forge themselves, interacting within and beyond our created contexts. They may choose to be happy and responsible or not, and by their own standards of both.

In the last analysis then, our finest parenting gift to our children is basically our moral example and our own authenticity. It reminds me of a teacher in Seattle who asked her class of fifth graders how many thought there would be nuclear war. All of the children, except one, raised their hands. The teacher was startled, but she was even more astonished that one child held out against all the others. So, she asked, "Why don't you agree, Carrie? And the little girl answered, "Because my Dad and Mom go to a meeting every Tuesday night, so that there won't be war anymore!"

An eighth parental reminder: remain patient. The Hebrew

word for patience stems from an idiom that means to "carry a heavy load," and in Tibetan, it's *bzod pa*, which means steadfastness and equanimity in the face of difficulties. Patience is not passive; it's not coasting or lounging around. It comes from the Latin *patior* which means "to suffer," denoting the human ability to bear misfortune or pain without complaint. It's an active virtue requiring outer and inner effort, fearlessness, and ample fortitude. If that doesn't paint the oft-burdensome task of parenting, I don't know what does.

The word compassion could be read as *com-patience*, because the terms passion and patience both find their roots in the same Latin word, *pati*. True patience is the opposite of lingering where we let things happen and allow others to make the decisions. Patience means to enter slowly but unwaveringly into the thicket and fully to bear (as well as *bare*) the suffering, joy, and anger therein, certainly omnipresent in the profession of parenting. Patience hangs tough and endures. It obliges us to practice the way of compassion.

There's a beautiful expression in the Christian scriptures that appears only twelve times. That phrase is "to be moved with compassion." The Greek verb *splangchnizomai* reveals the deep and powerful meaning of this term. The *splangchna* are the entrails of the body, or as we might say today, the innards. They're the place where our most intimate and intense emotions are faced. I've yet to meet any parent who isn't endowed with *splangchna* and consistently called upon to use them.

But compassionate parenting is even more complicated, because there are obviously moments when *impatience* is called for. To nudge our offspring toward necessary development, we fathers and mothers occasionally have to display irritation or displeasure.

A final parenting challenge: all children matter.

Our children are neither more precious nor more important than other children, but are reminders of the world's children.
—Liz and Philip Berrigan

We parents like to view our children as select and special creatures. Of course, they're dear to us, often residing among our most precious blessings. Furthermore, if we don't appreciate our own offspring, then chatter about caring about children abroad in the world rings hollow.

However, the Berrigans are nudging us to remember that adults must create spheres of justice and mercy beyond our households. I know of an after-school mentoring program called "They're All My Kids!" which echoes my sentiment here. We need to demonstrate our kinship with the little and helpless, innocent and growing children in every land and every era, accepting Abraham's charge in Genesis 12:3, "we strive to live as a blessing for all the families of the earth."

In the Masai warrior culture, the inevitable daily greeting, adult to adult, is: "and how are the children of the village?" signaling that the barometer of a society's well-being is how its younger ones are being treated and doing. Are they being fed properly, cared for regularly, and given hope for shaping promising and just tomorrows? I'll never forget visiting one of our church teenagers who had been abused and was living in a "safe center" for women and children. Above the door as one entered the house were found these words: "Remember, children are meant to be heard and listened to and believed!" Absolutely!

The staggering fact is that the average time we adults spend shopping per week is six hours and the average time we spend playing with our own children is forty minutes. And things are getting worse: the reduced time parents spend with their offspring today compared to 1965: 40%.

If there's one unmistakable truth resident in the ministry of the Galilean rabbi, it was his push for a better status for the marginalized of society, especially the lost, the powerless, and the little ones. We would do well to heed his literal exhortation to "let the children come up to me and do not try to stop them," recorded in Mark, Matthew, and Luke. And the Nazarene was referring to all the earth's youngsters—children we will never know personally, children from foreign lands, children who stagger and reel on life's edges, and children not yet born.

Geoffrey Canada, Harlem activist-educator, challenges any of us who are desirous of reviving civilization, to advance one step at a time, one person at a time: "You never know what will save or lose a child, so save the child close to you." And if you can't save them, at least be willing to serve them.

Tribal wisdom would gather and call in the elders, seasoned cradlers of the entire hamlet, weighing us with one charge: help bring to spiritual maturation yet another child. We seniors are "soulfully gifted," as my friend puts it, since we've weathered innumerable heartaches and satisfactions. Now's the season to pass our gifts along.

You and I may never attain the stature of *shaman* (wizened link with the spirit world), *tzaddik* ("righteous one"), *sanyasi* (religious ascetic) or *bodhisattva* (assisting one and all in the quest for enlightenment). An achievable role is becoming embodied elders, precisely where we're planted, as the elder tree has done with its purple berries.

There's a glorious passage in Jewish lore, where Abraham visits his great-grandfather, Shem. The elder gives the younger bread and wine, followed by some counsel:

Abraham, my dear one, if you wish to convert the world to Yahweh, surely a worthy mission, you must give folks both bread and wine, the old must be connected to the new, so both can remain vital. On the one hand, bread is clearly best when it's fresh; on the other hand, the older wine is, the better it becomes.

Shem's right on purpose. In order to create the kind of universe of which every age bracket can be duly proud, bread and wine must be offered in tandem; youngsters and seniors need to join hearts and hands. Generational spanning is time never squandered. My mind is sharper, my soul thicker, and my conscience broader whenever I spend time with children and youth. For love, at its base, is spelled T-I-M-E.

Are you familiar with the bumper sticker that reads: "The most radical thing we can do is introduce people to one another!" This constitutes sound wisdom and is downright germane for generational bridging. The window of time young and old share in common passes by quickly, the gulf remains vast, and the hunger is profound. We owe one another not so much a piece of our minds (although that's part of the bargain) but rather a huge portion of our energy and our embrace. We owe one another what American journalist, H. L. Mencken (1880-1956), called "a terrible loyalty"— terrible as in urgent and daunting yet enjoyable.

Marc Freedman, CEO of *Encore, org.,* has written a recent book called *How to Live Forever: The Enduring Power of Connecting the*

Generations which sports an unmistakable thesis: if seniors want to live forever, then we need to spend more quality time with younger folks, swapping notes and hopes. Lamentably, Freedman documents that only 1/3 of all elders exhibit a purpose beyond themselves. Our younger ones don't seek glad-handers or short-timers, marshmallows or reflections of themselves. They sorely clamor to be just who they are—children and youth—and they can best be such when we seniors are seniors: distinct yet equal abettors in creating a more just and joyful universe.

In intergenerational exchanges of respect and care, we're lighting one another's torches. We're *con-spiring*—"breathing together" more acutely than we could ever breathe alone. As an elder, I'm aspiring to plant seeds without being around for the harvest. We launch life within nuclear family units. We didn't earn or choose the ones we got; we inherited them. Our mission is to love our given families as honorably as we can, pledging a vow comparable to the following:

> *I promise to love, honor, and cherish*
> *all parts of myself and our family,*
> *in sickness and in health,*
> *for better, for worse,*
> *for richer, for poorer,*
> *till death do us part or unite*

But we don't stop there. We venture outward to forge chosen and extended families. Then we keep trekking to salute the "wholly family" of humanity. Our familial universe swells to embrace plants and animals and other earthly creatures. Family, at its fullest, becomes a cosmic household, ever-expanding to include yet one more presence or connection. As Douglas Steere (1901-1995), American Quaker ecumenist, keenly frames it: "God is always revising our boundaries outward."

So, here I reside, an elder moseying down my homestretch. I'm still a practicing parent, grandparent, and now great-grandparent, albeit from a distance, since five-year-old Kaliyah lives in Portland, Oregon. And when any of the youngers in my world might ask: "Hey, what did you do or who were you really?", I need to plumb deeper than mentioning family status or job achievements and try to illuminate the nubbins of my presence on earth with affirmations like this: "I've been a foibled yet joyful servant at home and in the larger world." Yes, that sentence fits fairly well. My key aspiration has been to become a "joyful servant!"

How about you, dear ones? How might you sum up your life for the generations coming on ahead?

> **Study questions for personal reflection and/or group discussion**

(1) In what fashion have you been able and willing to *honor* your parents, each of them? Be specific.

(2) Honestly, depict what kind of child you have been? Recall some of the ups and downs, trials and triumphs.

(3) How have you been or failed to be an honorable parent yourself?

(4) Describe times of forgiving and being forgiven in your family?

(5) Are there things still left to say, be, or do to enable your family bonds to be relationally current, cemented, and caring?

Chapter VI

Essential Sanctity of Life

VI. Thou shall not kill.
—Exodus 20:13

All things are our relatives.
—Henaka Sapa or Black Elk (1863-1950)

Sociologists tell us that the murder rate in modern society is less than at any time in our history including our lengthy period as hunter-gatherers. But they've not considered the possibility that humans have simply replaced physical violence with psychological and spiritual violence. Insulting, disdaining, shunning, and slandering have largely replaced beatings, but the damage is no less severe.
—Jeffrey Lockwood (1960-)

> *... My heart is moved by all I cannot save:*
> *So much has been destroyed.*
>
> *I have to cast my lot with those*
> *who age after age, perversely,*
>
> *with no extraordinary power,*
> *reconstitute the world.*
> —Adrienne Rich (1929-2012)

Life is our most precious possession. But when this noble and sweeping commandment is used in absolute form, "thou shalt not kill," we find it impossible to heed. For life feeds on life; we cannot help but kill to live. A close friend of ours, a staunch Buddhist, and consummate practitioner of the hallowed life, weeps whenever she squashes even a spider or ant.

And as I creep closer toward a more plant-based regimen, my vegan buddies remind me that even an herb-sodden diet causes some suffering. Whenever we pull or pick plants from the ground, their life-force is broken. We trigger trauma. For modern nutritional science notes that plants can communicate, grow connected, and are prone to take care of each other.

A family member recently nudged me to view the Discovery TDQ "nature documentary" (2013) titled: "What Do Plants Talk About?" The lessons are stunningly relevant to our realization of the 6th commandment. Despite having no eyes, ears, mobility or brains, plants still move and grow above and below ground, exhibiting complex feeding and foraging behavior. They become botanical vampires when seeking nutrients and suitable hosts. They're more predatory and animal-like than we ever conceived. Why? Because they want to live! What might this scientific evidence mean for our own behavior and the pertinence of #6. Well, like animals and humans, plants regularly both harm and help other life in order to survive. Plants balance positive and negative social interactions. They're cooperative with other plants as well as staunch competitors.

Scientific researchers summarize: "We humans aren't as smart as we thought we were, and plants are far more intelligent than we ever imagined." So, let's just sit and soak a moment, amidst these sobering and humbling facts. Sit and soak caringly, alongside plants and animals—our relatives.

When sufficiently settled of soul, we would refocus, narrowing the scope of the commandment to: thou shalt not kill persons. Put thusly, it reflects our deepest ethical impulses, and yet there may be instances when the refusal to ever kill humans can lead to worse hurt and destruction. Remember that prominent biblical figures—Moses, David, and Paul—are all guilty of breaking this commandment.

We must also note that Commandment #6 condemns the willful murder of the innocent but permits capital punishment. The Hebrew Scriptures call for the death penalty on numerous times.

I've been a peace activist all of my adult life: never choosing to serve in the military; counseling *Conscientious Objectors* throughout my ministry; co-founding, in 1984, San Diego's still-existent Peace Resource Center; and I can't see myself ever using weapons, let alone killing another person. Yet the older I get, the less easy my conscience rests with pure pacifism.

In most cases, murder is evil, yet global consensus would be that self-preservation sometimes overrides this commandment. Excruciating questions cascade: Are there times for self-defense? Are there not occasions when active euthanasia is appropriate? What about reproductive justice and the importance of abortion rights? Might there be values and causes worth killing or dying for? And garbled yeses pour forth from my conflicted soul.

And what about the uncomfortable issue of suicide? I retreat to my early ministry, back in 1970, when my friend and church member, Bob Cudney, in his late twenties, took a shotgun and killed himself.

When I heard of Bob's suicide, I quickly drove over to his wife's home. As Jeannette and I walked block after block after block, she recounted, in full detail, the events of recent weeks. She needed to cleanse her throbbing spirit. As Jeannette tried to unravel the explosive feelings that seemed to drive Bob to take his life, I broke down crying, and, I've wondered, both then and now, from whence cometh all my sobbing? Jeannette's mingled feelings of love, surprise, anger, guilt, and grief were far more intense than mine. Bob was a friend but not an intimate one. In truth, I was sobbing for Bob and for Jeannette, but I was also weeping for myself. His suicide had flung open the door of my own irrational, self-destructive impulses which both attracted and repelled me, but were closer to the surface than I realized.

Bob Cudney's death, by his own hand, reminded me that he wanted something badly but didn't know what it was or how he might reach it. Instead Bob found and built walls, ones he wasn't strong or sharp enough to scale. And then I realized: I know some of that struggle too, and so do other members of humanity! Bob's suicide led me to affirm, once again, that life was more important for its depth than its length, its quality than its quantity. And some of us get in more living in a few years than others get in many. Was that the case for Bob? Is that true for me and you?

The rage, the frustrations, and the impotence which propelled Bob to commit suicide have sometimes rattled and immobilized our lives too. What destroyed him also bothers us, at least, momentarily. Bob loved life, not all of it, but who does? He enjoyed portions of existence and wanted to hang in there, but not as he currently experienced it. He felt trapped in an unbearable box and didn't possess the emotional wherewithal to get out of it. Or so he believed. Hence, he ceased his present life. In killing his miserable now-self, Bob killed himself for all future moments. Bob Cudney chose to take his life; even as you and I might choose to keep ours.

Psychiatrist Karl Menninger (1893-1990) was discerning when he offered: "In the end, each person kills themselves in their own selected way, fast or slow, soon or late." You and I are often indulging in suicide on the installment plan, and if we're surprised when it's suddenly paid up in full, we shouldn't be. We all know the particular ways in which we might carry on borderline, desperate lives.

The line between suicide and non-suicide is often thin and delicate. Suicide is a temptation and an option. For the sick person in a severely wretched body or shriveled soul, is suicide right? For the elderly anticipating rebirth with loved ones on the far side of death, is it understandable? When is it noble and when is it ignoble to commit suicide? Only you and I can answer those questions. The right to live implies the right to end life, and the right of self-determination includes the right of self-termination. Suicide is a grizzly, byzantine moral decision.

There's more to be addressed in commandment #6. We moderns are impelled to face *other* subtle forms of destruction, even accidental wounding, which we commit. Lockwood's analysis is convincing: we humans are adept perpetrators of all sorts of mayhem and devastation, deliberate or inadvertent. Even some of the best of our mortal lot have displayed a checkered character.

Albert Schweitzer (1875-1965), renowned theologian, consummate organist, and dutiful humanitarian bore a blemished behavioral record. He won the 1952 Nobel Peace Prize for his philosophy of "Reverence for Life." He exhibited a consistent desire not to kill any living being: crocodiles, rats, even mosquitoes. Yet his attitudes toward the Africans with whom he worked, in retrospect, were colonialist, even racist. And Schweitzer was reported to have occasionally struck his co-workers, when they showed sluggishness on the job. As Xan Smiley, editor at Large for the *Economist* inquires: "Can a racist also be a virtuous person?" I say: "Yes. What would your verdict be?"

Oskar Schindler (1908-1974) was a German Catholic business man and confidant of the Nazis, who, during the Holocaust, protected and rescued some 1,200 Jews from almost certain death. In Poland today, where Schindler once ran his profitable enamelware factory during World War II, there are fewer than 4,000 Jews left. Around the world there are more than 6,000 descendants of the "Schindler Jews" he saved. Nobody can say with certainty what made this improbable hero risk his life when so many others failed to lift a finger. Was it guilt, greed, goodness, or a combination thereof?

Schindler was a hedonist of the highest order: a heavy drinker and a compulsive gambler. He was also a congenial man who may have been motivated by nothing more complicated than decency. In sum, Oskar Schindler was neither a saint nor a scoundrel, but an intractable mixture of both. His ambivalent character is what makes this story relevant to everyone who is also flawed yet committed to the grueling tussle of creating a harmonious world. In Schindler's life, as in our own lives, the sentiment of the African Roman playwright, Terence (185-159 BC) rings true: "Nothing human is alien to us." There exists nothing that is either hideous or holy that is foreign to our nature.

And what about Mahatma ("Great Soul") Gandhi (1869-1948) the renowned East Indian lawyer who led his country to freedom from British colonial rule in 1947? It's tempting to turn moral sages like Gandhi into unattainable saints. Deified, Gandhi can always be dismissed as a remote idealist; humanized, his life begs to be studied and his nonviolence to be pursued. Gandhi often reminded his companions that there's nothing he was accomplishing that another person could and should not aspire to accomplish. Gandhi, like Mother Teresa, and countless other exemplars, was an earthbound creature, who, like ourselves, is beset with handicaps and imperfections.

As a partner and parent, Gandhi was deficient. He was married at the age of thirteen to Kasturbai, an unformed teenager as well. Their parents made the match but didn't tell them until wedding preparations were underway. The result: "two innocent children were unwittingly hurled on the ocean of life," with presumably only their experiences in a former incarnation to guide them. Gandhi later decried "the cruel custom of child marriage."

Their partnership was a stormy one, especially in the early years. Many times Mohan and Kasturbai wouldn't even speak to each other. Gandhi experienced moments of extreme jealousy over his wife and was a domineering, sometimes petulant, husband who felt it was his right to impose his will upon her.

Gandhi, in forming his *ashram*, had insisted on bringing "untouchables" into the household. Kasturbai had accepted this without complaint. She found it too much, however, when her husband required that she assume the job of removing their toilet wastes from the house, something he himself was unwilling to do. Gandhi later confessed: "I was a cruelly kind husband. I regarded myself as her teacher and harassed her out of my blind love for her." I'm not sure his love was blind, so much as grievously stunted and insensitive.

Gandhi was also an incompetent father to his four sons. Expecting them to be junior saints, Gandhi denied them a formal education on the grounds that character was more critical than learning and a profession in public service. Gandhi's oldest son, in a frantic bid to be free, became everything his father was not: a meat eater, a drinker of alcohol, a gambler, and a convert to Islam. He wound up embezzling money. Gandhi paid the sum back, then printed an account of the affair in his newspaper, *Young India*, concluding that "people may be good, but not necessarily their children." Regrettably, it was easier for Gandhi to love disciples than his own progeny—those folks afar more than those nearby. He used to say: "All India is my family." In truth, his country was more his family than his own wife and offspring. This is a dreadful yet oft-common plight for public leaders.

In our Western world, we exhibit a tendency toward dichotomies. You are either good or evil, nothing in between. Hindu religion is subtler; everything in existence is a mixture of both;

therefore, their aim, although not necessarily their accomplishment, is, whenever possible, to let the good predominate. This is reflected in the marvelous myth of Narakarasura, on whose birthday *Divali*, the notable fall festival of India, is celebrated. In Hindu lore, Narakarasura was an evil demon, but he was also the son of the great preserver-god, Vishnu. Narakarasura was by no means all bad. He did much good in his life, and for a long while the good predominated.

However, he became an increasingly evil influence, and when the evil began to outweigh the good, Vishnu decreed that his son must die. "But," protested Narakarasura: "Don't the scriptures say that good follows good as evil follows evil?" "Yes," said Vishnu, "that's correct." "Then what do I get for the good I have done?" asked Narakarasura. "What do you think you should get?" asked Vishnu. "I think," said Narakarasura slyly, "that when you celebrate the triumph of good over evil, you should do it on my birthday!" And, that is why the festival of *Divali* falls on the birthday of an evil demon.

Divali would remind us that, in the long run, the best solution is to proclaim an armistice and welcome the warring factions into the human commonwealth. Opposites belong together; dualisms can be bridged; and the contradictions of each and every life need to be encompassed or clasped in creative tension.

Here's yet another narrative on the abiding ambivalence of human nature. Thich Nhat Hanh, the skillful practitioner of peaceful crusading, in his powerful poem: *Call Me by My True Names*, confesses, in a pirate's murdering of a young girl on a boat during the Vietnam War, that he is ...

> *the 12-year-old girl, the pirate, as well as himself. Can we look at each other and recognize ourselves in each other. I have many names, when I hear one of these names, I have to say Yes! When I am able to see that I am all these people, my hatred disappears, and I can live to help the victim and the perpetrators.*

I'd like to agree with Hanh that our hatred disappears, but very few of us resemble the level of this Buddhist monk's self-realization. Someone has noted, "Hatred is a normal neurosis." When used discreetly, it can be a way of resisting personal wrong or social terror and of drawing limits when human dignity is threatened. However, we must use hate judiciously, lest it devour the hater and annihilate the target. There's a time to hate, but then a time to release from the hatred and move toward truce. As the *Dhammapada*, sacred Buddhist scripture, exhorts: "Hatred never ceases by hatred, but by love alone is healed. This is an ancient and eternal law." What seems prudent is to love boldly and hate mindfully.

Can we, at least, admit that we engage in cruelties? As my colleague, The Rev. Dr. William Schulz, who served as the Amnesty International Director, dealing regularly with gross human rights violations and war crimes, soberly puts it:

> *Cruelty is real. Along with intimations of goodness, evil lies coiled in almost every human heart, latent in almost every human enterprise. The goal is not to vanquish it, but to temper it, and naming it is always the first step toward its taming.*

No unsophisticated commandment, # 6. It's loaded with sneaky minefields and problematic standards.

On the one hand, there is the iron necessity of nature that life kills to live. On the other hand, is the humane commandment "thou shalt not kill." So, here's where I end up. An essential sanctity attaches to all life, including animal and plant life, and, it's suitable to violate that sanctity only when the failure to violate it would likely lead to graver violence. How can we develop *biophilia*, an affinity for the entire living world, not just other human beings? Vegetarians don't eat anything with a face, and each of us must draw a line, to reduce suffering; yet it's in our nature to destroy life someway, sometime, somewhere.

I resonate with the perceptiveness of Buddhist practitioner, Diane Eshin Rizzetto:

> *Over time, what we come to realize is that to live means to take life and to take life means to live. Every time we drink water to hydrate our body we kill millions of micro-organisms. Every time we take a refreshing walk across the sweet green grass in the park, we kill innumerable tiny creatures. We cannot escape taking life so that we can survive, and at the same time we can support life in whatever ways we can.*
>
> *See what life comes into our field of vision. Say quietly to yourself: "you are life; I am life; we are life." You will find that it is impossible to find a place without life. Begin to notice what offers its life to support your life. Consider the ways in which you support life. Try to keep it simple and ordinary.*

Therefore, may I dedicate myself never to injure life except in the necessary interest of life. May I come humbly to every choice I make, be it abortion, animal and plant rights, capital punishment, suicide, or warfare. May I never kill with impunity but with a sense of regret and grief. May I remain vigilant not just about killing the body but killing the mind and the spirit of others as well as within my own self ... what is termed "inner killing."

And may I aspire to be kind-hearted around murderers, because they, like you and I, were once babies (even if often unloved and abused). May I consider everyone to be a singular and worthwhile being. Don't we all deserve some level of restorative rather than retributive justice when our overall journeys are evaluated?

My brother and his wife have worked for years at the San Quentin prison in Northern California, counseling young adult murderers, who committed their slayings in their teens and have been given life-sentences. They're currently trying to redeem themselves and hopefully return as healthy, contributing members of society. The Kid-Cat program was formed by members of the prison population to prioritize accountability in the lives of these teenagers and young adults. First and foremost, they must embrace fully their horrific crimes while not being doomed to an identity as a permanent criminal. "I committed my crime, but I am not my crime."

Many inmates, after years of strenuous rehab, are able to re-instate their lives through the *Kid-CAT* program and re-enter the public world. Phil and Gail seek to embody the compassionate philosophy of Sister Helen Prejean (1939-):

> With death-row inmates, it's always about presence. I'm here to be here for you and to hold out before you your dignity as a child of God. It's that presence and constancy and fidelity to people that's the most that I can give them. Then I introduce them sometimes to others or even just tell stories of people I

know and what they've done. But I never set myself up to be a healer to people who have endured a pain that I have never endured.

Let us refuse to kill the dignity of any other human being. We may condemn the deed but never the worth of the doer. Let us treat every day as an opportunity to practice as much reverence for life as our soul impels.

Killing takes other forms than just physical; we earthlings can kill intellectually, emotionally, socially, and religiously as well. We are susceptible to murderous speech. Animosity often leads to demolishing relationships, ideas, and possibilities. Bitterness can result in acts of revenge. Malice, of any variety, can drive us back into slavery. As Nelson Mandela (1918-2013), the renowned South African politician, imprisoned 26½ years for his courageous activism, stated, after ultimately forgiving his captors:

*Resentment is like drinking poison
and then hoping it will kill our enemies.*

Resentment is a diminishing and destructive human emotion.

We demonstrate an array of sadistic attitudes and brutal behaviors, both local and global, and all are rooted in violations of personhood. Robert McAfee Brown (1920-2001), Protestant theologian and activist, reminds one and all:

When we talk about a person, we are not talking about an object but about a subject. We are describing someone who is not quantifiable or interchangeable with another. Each person has unique worth.

As a religious movement unequivocally committed to the dignity of the L.G.B.T.Q.I.A. community since the early 1970's, Unitarian Universalists are horrified by the rise in the number of anti-L.G.B.T.Q. bills (some 400 plus new ones across the United States) and vicious gender identity policing. Just recently, Florida governor, Ron DeSantis, signed legislation that banned gender transition care for minors and prohibited public school officials from asking children their preferred pronouns. And once such laws stand on the books, it's well-nigh impossible to remove them. Understandably, our *Human Rights Campaign* has declared it a state of emergency.

We dwell in a land where bigotry is becoming normalized! Desmond Tutu (1931-2021), South African Anglican bishop and anti-apartheid activist, rightly claimed: "If you are neutral in situations of injustice, you have chosen the side of the oppressor." Commandment #6 requires us to fight unremittingly, across borders, for inclusion, diversity, and equity for all.

When Thucydides (460-400 B.C.) was asked if justice would ever come to Athens, the Greek general and historian replied, "Justice will not come to Athens until those who are not injured are as indignant as those who are injured." That ancient contention still rings true in the craggy, steep battle for justice and dignity in our 21st century. Now is no era to wallow in neutrality, spectating from the sidelines, because of our age or condition. Instead, it's the season to continue breaking silence and joining the resistance, to keep listening to the sound of harm and raising a righteous ruckus. We are called to be life-long allies, accomplices, and advocates for everyone who suffers injustice.

An elder of the Achuar tribe of Ecuador, one of the oldest indigenous peoples of South America, upon being offered help by a well-intentioned Westerner, responded in this way:

> *If you've come to help me, you're wasting your time.*
> *But if you've come because your liberation is tied up*
> *with mine, then we can work together.*

We're not done with this comprehensive and convoluted commandment. Let's now make a case for *anger*.

Anger is one of the most essential emotions we ever experience. We get angry with those who matter most to us. Apathy, not anger, is the opposite of love. If we don't care about someone, we don't risk strong, let alone negative, feelings. Anger-with-heart puts fire into any alliance: a fire that burns, cleanses, destroys, and heals in service of relational well-being.

Anger alerts us to the fact that something is missing or gone awry in our friendship. Anger draws boundaries and creates space within our intimate bonds. An honest relationship is never filled merely with sweetness and light.

Children often grow up with rare displays of constructive outrage modeled by the adults in our world. That was certainly the case in my own household. Therefore, children come to believe a batch of unhelpful platitudes like: "If you display anger, then you don't love me," or "tame your rage, then convert it into a quick and huge smile," or "if you have to get mad, then at least do it politely."

On the contrary, feeling angry is a human phenomenon as universal as feeling hungry or tired, lonely or happy. The situations that make us angry, the ways we grow furious, and the things we do when we are incensed are not the same. Some who are angry may *break* a pot; others will *make* a pot. It all depends.

Lamentably, we can fall prey to the harmful extremes of slow-burning bitterness or all-consuming fury. Suppressed anger can result in insomnia, high blood pressure, fatigue, habitual sarcasm, gastro-intestinal disorders, and headaches. Verbal or physical outbursts of anger are also deleterious to social health, either alienating or escalating a normal conflict into all-out strife.

The challenge is to release our anger for *impact* rather than venting our hostility for *injury*, for setting bounds rather than for bashing. There are no pat formulas or undemanding solutions, but a handful of measures are in order.

First, we need to recognize that we're angry. If we are tense or dejected, we inquire: what is bothering us? At whom are we harboring upset? We never need to justify anger. Feelings are facts. Getting angry is neither right nor wrong; it just is.

Second, when possible, identify the source of the anger. To deal with our ire, we must locate the real cause, internal or external or a blend of the two; then, we possess the acumen to release our anger on target.

Third, we need to cope with our anger realistically. This calls us to deal with small irritations by discussing them openly, before they accumulate and produce painful division. There's wisdom in the biblical injunction that lovers not let the sun go down on our anger. That was Carolyn's and my marital mantra and mission, although we sometimes fell short.

Fourth, we need to establish agreeable rituals for handling anger. Whenever one person I know, feels fury bubbling up inside, she lets her beloved know that she has to discharge some rage from her system. He agrees that she can let loose with a verbal tirade, usually for a few minutes. The anger is released with his non-defensive support, so it is less likely to do any damage. Once the heat is off, the two set a future time to talk through the issue.

Another insight. Just as it takes two to tango, so it takes two to tangle. Whether you, your companion, or your child is the initiator, any legitimate conflict belongs to the two of you. It is tempting to scapegoat; but the truth is that fights can only be resolved when we both realize our culpability and labor to bridge the gulf.

In sum, conflict signals the price of tender, growing friendship or intimacy. It's possible to express anger without attacking the other person's ego. Not easy to be sure, but easy is usually another name for withdrawal, revenge, or compliance. Those who are angry stick close enough to solve arguments and exhibit respectfulness. They find ways to be angry together.

There's more to unscramble regarding #6. I seek to follow the intricate art of saying *Yes* to aggression and *No* to violence. We must become a species daring enough—make that aggressive enough—to blow the whistle on the escalating, gratuitous violence across our land. We must cease and counter any and all violations of personhood and property we continue to commit. As II Timothy 1:7 urges: "God did not give us a spirit of timidity, but a spirit of power and love and self-control."

Aggression isn't a horrid word at root. It literally means moving forward: toward a person, a posture, a principle, or an event. It references eluding the grasp of lethargy or fright and advancing toward our goal. We humans need to aggress what we value: to move toward someone in regard; to move away into nourishing solitude; to move against something in opposition. Of course, there will be dangers to dodge. Our regard dare not breed docility. Our solitude can't slide into seclusion. Our opposition must avoid recklessness. But aggression is the ground floor, animating energy that undergirds brave, forward-moving deeds.

Whereas violence destroys; aggression can create, heal, and bridge ... producing personal growth and substantive social change. There's a case to be made for the necessary gift of benign aggression. Speaking as a self-identified man, I need to outgrow groveling niceness, faintheartedness of conscience, and spongy backbone ... in short, cowardice. We males must develop, then practice, kindly aggression in order to thicken our maturation.

As one committed, since the early 1970's, to becoming a more emotionally-expressive, ethically-worthy, and ecologically-responsible man, through organizing and participating in mature men's movements, let me share some concrete examples of humane male-to-male aggression.

One of the healthiest, non-invasive actions we can take is to massage one another's back and hands. We've done back-to-back massages in a train-line early on in men's gatherings, but hand-to-hand massaging requires more time and trust. Yet whenever we've invited men to knead another man's hands in caring way, not only is it relaxing and calming, but it also often represents the first time most men have ever caressed another brother's hands.

After the hand massage, we grant men time to talk about this physically intimate exchange, and abundant tears and heartfelt confessions consistently flow. Men's hands, softened by this simple exercise, are now strengthened to stroke others in soothing, non-injurious ways.

Countless men have forthwith chosen to place in their wallets a pledge, crafted by our *UU Men's Fellowship* member, Tomas Firle, who suffered Nazi violence himself while growing up in Germany.

His oath charges us to employ our hands for embraces, wringing, creativity, gardening, car repair, baking, caressing, defiance, and play, but never for damage.

The card reads.

My Interpersonal No-Violence Pledge

I SHALL NOT:
- *raise my voice or use threats to dominate others*
- *raise my hands in an intimidating manner*
- *hit or hurt anyone, physically or emotionally, to get my way*

INSTEAD I SHALL:
- *seek help when I feel moved to the point of violence*
- *speak out when I witness abuse by others*
- *encourage others to take an active stand against violence*
- *use my hands for healing not harm*

Then we sign our names at the bottom. I find it morally invigorating to have such a card butting up against family photos, credit cards, and other wallet miscellany as a constant reminder of what's truly important in my quest to become a more fulfilled male being.

We now migrate from reinterpreting aggression in a positive manner to ascertaining the resourcefulness of nonviolence when engaging the 6th commandment. It's a philosophy which, although infrequently heralded or honored in America, is as old as history itself. From ancient times to the present, people have renounced violence as a means of resolving disputes. They've opted instead for aggressive negotiation, mediation, and reconciliation, resisting violence with an uncompromising regard for the integrity of all human beings—friends and enemies alike.

Mahatma Gandhi called it *satyagraha*—"soul or truth force." He contended that every conflict or problem whether among family or friends, communities or governments, or inside our very own conscience, will be addressed, in the final analysis, either through violent or nonviolent force. Those who choose nonviolence, opt for the force of justice, the force of love, the force of redistributing power and privilege, the force of non-cooperation, the force of relentless resistance to evil, and the force of imaginative, revolutionary ideas. *Satyagraha*.

The non-violent pilgrim acknowledges and affirms the full humanity of every person and refuses to be vengeful. However, when we pursue the non-violent path, we'll inevitably run into those who voice "but what if ..." scenarios. Arguments against nonviolence are often about impossible situations where violence wouldn't work either. There's considerable irony in the presumed compassion of a questioner who is so concerned about the potential rape of a single grandmother but also accepts war, in which the rape of grandmothers, wives, daughters, and children is so routine that many soldiers have considered rape to be one of the compensations of warfare.

Certainly, there exist situations that are crushingly tragic, where nothing we can conceivably do will help. Holding hands and singing "give peace a chance" doesn't stop warlords from stealing food from starving babies. There are times when the violent and nonviolent alike are forced to suffer the agony of irrelevance and may themselves reside among the victims.

Terrorism and war are rampant throughout the world, and at home, even as I tearfully pen these words. My soul is torn to pieces over the heedless and brutal war that Russia has perpetrated against Ukraine or the horrible bloodshed in the Middle East between Hamas and the Israelis.

Furthermore, there's nothing magical about nonviolence. It requires courage and demanding work, immense self-discipline, and a well-integrated spirituality. It entails the willingness to maintain an open mind and to learn from our enemies. Yes, even from our enemies. And it necessitates the ability to desire their safety as well as our own, to understand the part in them that tries to hurt others, even while refusing to cooperate with it.

And no matter how nonviolent we purport to be in theory or practice, we must never envision evil as if it were something arising outside ourselves. We must confess our complicity in the very evils we abhor. Self-righteousness is a deceptive and treacherous sin. All our creative and compassionate philosophizing regarding commandment #6, "thou shalt not kill," means nothing unless we choose to be peacemakers, first and foremost, within our very own hearts and households.

As the Psalmist (122:7) says: "May peace dwell within your walls." But we can't halt there. Don't hide or hoard your peacefulness within your own heart or home; go forth and spread it, generously and universally, throughout the course of your one, holy and priceless, life.

May our humble prayer become:

Eternal Spirit of Life, Love, and Liberation ...
*   prod us daily to become peace-pursuers and*
*   peace-producers ... here, there, and everywhere.!*

Shalom, salaam, ashay, namaste, blessed be, and amen!

Study questions for personal reflection and/or group discussion

(1) Name some of the ways you have done harm, been cruel or violent, or taken life ... intentionally or unintentionally? And don't forget instances of psychological and social harm.

(2) If you are a vegetarian or a vegan, explain why? If not, why not?

(3) Are there principles worth killing or dying for? If so, what?

(4) What are your feelings and thoughts about suicide?

(5) Describe examples of how you are inclined to kill/deaden the spirit of others as well as your own spirit?

(6) What does the phrase "nothing human is alien to me" mean to you?

(7) How do you find ways to be angry together in your daily engagements?

(8) How do you handle your bouts with resentment and hatred?

(9) Delineate ways in which you practice the art of kindly aggression?

(10) Explain when and where you show yourself to be an intentionally non-violent person?

Chapter VII

Treat All Relationships Respectfully

VII. Thou shall not commit adultery
—Exodus 20:14

We can never undo what we have done. We can never go back in time. Repentance—t'shuvah—is like the Japanese art of kintsugi, repairing broken pottery with gold. You can never unbreak what you have broken. But with the sincere and deep work of transformation, acts of repair have the potential to make something new.
—Rabbi Danya Ruttenberg (1975-)

I was an adulterer in my first marriage.

My misbehavior ceased after committing to a healthy and egalitarian marriage with Carolyn. I can't undo my harmful past, but I can work on transforming it. My present partnership has aspired to become a "phoenix rising out of the ashes."

Maybe you and you and you, along with me, have committed adultery as well. One-third of Americans currently claim to have cheated on a partner while in a monogamous relationship—either physically, emotionally, or both. However, numbers of people doing so doesn't make it okay. Commandment #7 is broken every time we fall prey to reckless or insensitive sexual expression and intentionally harm our primary partner as well as multiple family units. We live in an adulterous era, and adultery is a sin.

Healthy sexual communion furnishes a difficult blessing, because it requires time, commitment, and surrender. In the Song of Solomon we read this quintessential passage of love: "You are my beloved and you are my friend!" (5:16) For partners who are equally friends and beloveds, the sexual experience can be a continual renewal of their sense of unity, one of life's enduring joys.

What does it mean "to make love?" To be sure, lovers make noise, gyrations, and sometimes babies, but love is more mysterious and expansive than the result of any physical behavior. During mutually beneficial sexuality, more love is made than existed before the given partners dared the intimacies of erotic communion. Love is not made from scratch or in a vacuum, but rather created from gracious gifts, grown afresh within a secure and supportive context, activated by common respect and bedrock loyalty, and bathed in imagination, trust, and gawkiness. Indeed, the Inuit people's term for making love means "to make laughter together." So, we don't fall in love or even find it. We *make* love, and in so doing, such intimacy may bring us as close to God as we'll ever get. In fact, the Hebraic word for "knowing" Yahweh is the same term employed when sexually "knowing" your partner.

To celebrate their 50th wedding anniversary, a couple returned to their honeymoon hotel. After retiring, the husband said, "Darling, do you remember how you stroked my hair?" And so she stroked his hair. She reminded him of the way they cuddled, and so they did. With a sigh, she said, "Won't you nibble my ear again?" With that, the husband got out of bed and left the room. "Where are you going?" cried the upset wife. "To get my teeth!" her loving mate retorted.

Here, Carolyn and I, reside, in our own 50th year of marriage, aiming to nibble on each other's ears, all the way home ... while avoiding entanglement with our respective hearing aids.

Of course, the complexity of human love in today's world can't be painlessly handled by this 7th commandment. Moderns are increasingly less willing to live loveless lives or endure abusive bonds. Might not saving actual self-love be more germane than saving our marriage? And, adultery, in a profound sense, is a private matter, not something for public legislation or tribal law. Furthermore, the Nazarene, in the Christian scriptures, cautions us to quit tossing rocks at adulterers or anyone else. Take the rocks home and brew some stone soup for either your family or nearby neighbors.

One thing I've learned, over my ministerial career, is this: never hastily criticize the inner life or choices of another person, couple, or family. Relationships are singular and complicated. Judging can be a harsh and often useless response. I pay serious attention to the biblical admonition in Matthew (7:1, 3):

> *Judge not, that you be not judged. Why do you see the speck that is in your neighbor's eye but do not notice the log that is in your own eye?*

It's human nature to miss or minimize our own poverties of character while swift to note those of our neighbors. We do this not from confidence but insecurity. However, when we spend a good deal of time damning, there isn't a whole lot of energy left with which to love mercy, be kind, and do justice. Branches or shingles, specks or logs, the size of the wood isn't at issue.

The real concern of this biblical challenge is to urge humans to spend our moments cleaning up our own houses rather than ogling at the messes in the abodes of others. Anne McCaffrey's (1926-2011) line holds us in fine stead: "Make no judgments where you have no compassion."

The prime antidote to adultery is *fidelity*, an old-fashioned virtue which signals allegiance and faithfulness. I seek to resemble the words of naturalist Scott Russell Sanders (1945-), American novelist and personal essayist:

> *In speaking about marriage and other partnerships, I don't mean habit. I don't mean trudging along in a rut. I mean actively choosing, over and over, to stay on a path, to abide in a relationship, to answer a call. The sort of commitment I have in mind is compounded of stubbornness, affection, and wonder. My short-hand term for it is fidelity.*

Fidelity is a short-hand term that works well for the long-term. Commandment #7 claims that fidelity (faithfulness) remains the most fulfilling way to mature a relationship of primacy and intimacy. Fidelity entails paying deep and earnest attention to one another. Most of us are trained to love in bursts but falter over the long haul. While the juices flow and enthusiasm blazes, we love passionately. But love demands more continuity. It would have us carefully attend during the lulls and snags of our bonds. It calls for faithfulness.

Committed individuals must also recognize the nefarious forms of infidelity. Infidelity can occur whenever either lover breaks communication or sabotages closeness. Illicit, passionate attachments can estrange us. She/he/they lust after knowledge and lose self in books, precisely when the other yearns to talk. One romances sports, as participant and spectator, as an evasion of personal time with their precious companion.

The forms of unfaithfulness are sneaky and varied. I found that almost any excessive habit of mine could yank me away from time well-spent with Carolyn. A friend of ours, whose partner smokes against their will, moans: "It's as though there exists another lover in our house, a lover who pleases my beloved in mysterious ways I cannot."

We need not pummel ourselves over our peccadillos and transgressions. That's too easy. But we would do well to acknowledge that we go a-whoring, whenever our habits are unduly selfish, whenever we treat something or someone else as more important than our primary bond, whenever shared trust is battered or lost, and whenever we skirt or shun engagement with our beloved.

Furthermore, in a healthy partnership it's crucial to remember that our main mission is to *change thyself*. Numerous lovers tussle to control, even transform, the other. That's futile behavior. A partner's job is to make the necessary alterations in one's own being, and if our heart-mate is also refining their character and conduct, then interpersonal maturity can result.

When we take responsibility for our own part of any difficulty or disharmony, the burden is lightened, sometimes lifted, and the problem can usually be worked out through mutual understanding. Forget a total makeover; labor on adjusting a modest percentage of what you do and who you are ... as a committed partner. Consider changing 5% of your own habits.

Here's the scenario I like to hear when counseling couples: "You know what? My partner isn't meeting my expectations, and I'm unhappy. So I've chosen to become the kind of person whom she would more likely want to love, enjoy, and like ... and now, voila, I'm much happier!" The key to relational fulfillment is not so much finding the right mate as *being* the right person!

Our friend and skillful couples' therapist, Dr. Rebecca Cutter, always framed it this way: "We need to ask ourselves every morning questions such as: 'What was it like being partnered to me yesterday? What is something simple that I can do today that would make life easier for my lover? What is something that I already do that helps us as a couple? And am I willing to do that again tomorrow, even though it might not have been acknowledged that I did it today?'"

Here's additional counsel that buttresses the virtue of fidelity: the bravery to "go to the reef" when mutual growth is required. Eda LeShan (1922-2002), American writer, TV host, and educator, tells the story about a dinner party, when she sat next to a woman who was an oceanographer. At one point LeShan was asked if she had ever wondered why lobsters could weigh one pound, three pounds, even ten pounds when they had such a hard shell. How could they grow? Eda had to tell her dinner companion that resolving this fascinating quandary wasn't high on her list of priorities.

The woman smiled and proceeded to explain that when a lobster is crowded in its shell and can't grow anymore, it instinctively travels to some place in the sea, hoping for relative safety and begins to shed its shell. It's a terribly dangerous process—the lobster has to risk its life, because once it becomes naked and vulnerable, it could be dashed against a reef or eaten by another lobster or fish. But that's the only way it can grow.

Plenty of times, Carolyn and I, singly and as partners, have known that it was time "to go to the reef"—to grow and change, to become resourceful and buoyant, more of our best selves. We've experienced a nagging discontent with where and who we are that drives us to the reef, since staying in a tight shell spells certain stagnation.

One of my go-to passages for our own marriage has been from Proverbs 27:18: "As iron sharpens iron, so one person sharpens another." Contrary to popular belief, good friends and resilient couples bring their toughest stuff to the relational table. They don't pussyfoot around difficult emotions. They neither bully nor back off; rather they come on strong. Result: everybody involved emerges both sharpened and sharper.

Here's what a friend of ours, Esther, boldly states about her life-partner, Louise, of 27 years. "Sinewy of body, dogged by a low pain threshold, Louise's keen mind and emotional verve drew me to her and keep drawing me to her. In Louise's own way, she is steely and iron-like, and I've felt encouraged to display my emotional and moral muscle next to hers in our partnership." Esther and Louise are "as iron sharpens iron."

Another critical trait for a faithful partnership: avoid keeping score! I don't question for one minute the significance of equality in healthy bonds of intimacy. Egalitarianism has furnished the lodestar of our marriage. In fact, emblazoned on a small post in our abode are words from the American transcendentalist and women's rights activist, Margaret Fuller (1810-1850):

> *The highest form of marriage is men and women as equals on the pilgrimage of two souls toward a common shrine.*

But I've garnered a fresh insight over the years. It was brought home by one of our parishioners at her daughter's wedding.

I've been accustomed to calling our partnership a 50-50 proposition. Esmeralda told her daughter and son-in-law during the celebratory toasts to remember that there would be times when their marriage would be balanced, even egalitarian, but many times it would be a 90-10, 80-20, 75-25 percent enterprise. Her insight persuaded me. As partners, we won't, all the time, be equally involved emotionally, physically, financially, parentally, or socially. At any given moment, one of us might be called upon to carry a greater share of the relational freight. Is this not what Genesis 2:18 means when it calls upon us to be "helpmates?" Literally, helpmates are *mates* who *help* rather than patronize or ignore one another. Sometimes, we find our partner doing more of the helping. Other times, we're invited to take the lead. The delicate art is not to keep score.

Marriage isn't always a 50-50 blueprint. It's much more convoluted and varied than that, and partners need to stand ready to entertain different moods and flows, capacities and crises all the days of our loving. Put another way: responsibility in a solid partnership isn't a 50-50 arrangement but 100% of my being matched up with 100% of yours!

Our goal needs to be wholeness not perfection. Whole people long to be with whole people. Whole persons are willing to divulge their warts and weaknesses rather than hide them. They dance upon the razor's edge in pursuit of a loving bond. Whole people settle for a sufficiently good rather than a perfect match. Start by being the partner you wish to have.

In every case, whatever our relational circumstances might be, fidelity is required in our bonds of love. And fidelity costs energy, sacrifice, and time ... indeed, a lifetime.

The biblical equivalent of fidelity is *hesed* or loving-kindness, which is mentioned 245 times in the Hebrew Scriptures, conveying both an essential part of God's character as well as the nucleus of our human assignment. *Hesed* is more than a feeling or an attitude; it represents compassionate behavior. *Hesed* is kindness incarnated. And it doesn't refer to random, so much as intentional, acts of kindness. *Hesed* denotes deliberate behavior.

And kindness isn't the same as niceness. I believe in being polite and civil, but too much courtesy can degenerate into faintheartedness. There are moments, in stalwart bonds, when we should assert rather than defer, intervene and push back rather than submit. Kindness and fidelity are rugged and resilient qualities.

The kernel of this commandment wisely challenges humans, in all our friendships and loves, to be careful not to *adulterate*— corrupt, debase, make impure, shortchange, compromise, or sabotage—life's central vow of enduring loyalty and love. In sum, while this commandment to eschew adultery pertains specifically to safeguarding marriage, it's relevant to every bond which we fashion during our journeys. Commandment #7 charges one and all to be careful not to pollute or poison all human "intercourse." It summons us to choose fidelity over adultery in every relational choice and move we navigate.

Let me expand my reflections on commandment #7 with another core value that is a cousin to kindness and fidelity: *respectfulness*. Without the fortification of genuine respect, other noble virtues grow anemic. While love can turn mushy, respect remains brawny. When you respect a partner or stranger, friend or foe, you display unqualified regard and consideration.

There is perhaps no clearer depiction of what it means to treat strangers respectfully than in the Hebrew Scriptures:

> *Do not wrong or oppress a stranger, for you know what it feels like to be a stranger, for you yourselves were once strangers in the land of Egypt.*
> —Exodus 23:9

Rabbi Jonathan Sacks poignantly exegetes this text:

> *Note that this command is given shortly after the Exodus. Implicit is that radical idea that care for the stranger is why the Israelites had to experience exile and slavery before they could enter the Promised Land and build their own society and state. You will not succeed in caring for the stranger, implies God, until you yourselves know in your very bones and sinews what it feels like to be a stranger ...*

When America, along with countless other nations, is wrestling mightily with the complex challenges of immigration reform, we receive guidance from the Hebrew Scriptures where the phrase "love the stranger" appears some 36 times. Consequently, our social policies, however fashioned, are subpoenaed to be humane and hospitable. At our best, we're summoned not merely to tolerate the strangers but to welcome them. For all of us, as was true for the Israelites, at some point in our personal histories, have been strangers or immigrants. We've been considered outsiders, perhaps even aliens, and hankered to be treated with genuine regard or value ... to be respected.

Respect literally means "to look at something or someone again." Respectful persons are those who look again at what is easily ignored or missed. They look again at outworn, debilitating patterns and consider developing healthier habits. They look again at their own motives before casting aspersions on others. They repent of, then atone for, their own noxious attitudes and misbehaviors, whether intentional or not. Practitioners of respectfulness look again at our human history of gender disharmony and racial brutality ... aspiring to build a world of greater justice across lines of color and identity, class and orientation, conviction and capacity.

Any book freshly reframing the Ten Commandments must confront one of the largest elephants in the room: *patriarchy* or *toxic masculinity*. While granting self-identified men clout, patriarchy has caused costly, oft-irreparable damage to male bodies and souls—producing emotionally constipated boys, suicidal teenagers, miserable adults, and burgeoning violence against other males, females, trans, and non-binary folks. Patriarchy is based upon male exceptionalism and entitlement. Patriarchal society, pure and simple, worships and promotes gender domination—be it harassment, rape (and, remember, rape is approved in the Bible and the Greeks praised it), sexual assault, or the attack on women's health and bodily autonomy by removing basic coverage, cutting maternity care, or sharply limiting reproductive rights.

And, to worsen matters, Rabbi Rami Shapiro painfully notes that:

> *Clerical abuse of children is an evil rooted in masculine power, patriarchy, and the male God who supports and is supported by both. The Father-King-Lord-Shepherd God can reduce us to children, vassals, slaves, and sheep. Such surrender makes abuse of all kinds inevitable.*

The carnage continues.

Men need to muster the same kind of passion for combating patriarchy that we muster for technological gadgets, sports, wealth, cars, learning, wilderness escapades, professional achievement, romance and whatever else might capture our constancy. In battling patriarchy, we will be exhibiting *testosterone-with-heart*. But I harbor no illusions: in dismantling a tradition as entrenched as patriarchy, we will endure falling statuary as well as face considerable pushback from both men and women.

Recently, a poll by the Pew Research Center found that 56% of men and 34% of women thought that "sexism no longer was a barrier" to women in this country. Yes, over the past 50 years, overt sexism (like overt racism) has become less socially acceptable (certainly in progressive circles as well), but chauvinism is not dead. It's alive and kicking, shiftier and more pernicious than ever. As Jill Filipovic (1983-), American author and lawyer, acutely observes: "Hostile sexism is easy to identify and condemn. Benevolent sexism is more insidious."

We do not inhabit a post-sexist America, and current public rhetoric and behavior have had an effect of normalizing misogyny, just as it has mainstreamed anti-immigrant, anti-Semitic, and anti-Muslim sentiment.

Our male culture is riddled with patriarchy not merely a few bad apples. In this segment, I'm addressing males in particular, since that's my cisgender identity and the moral work I'm called to do. I can neither speak for nor craft the agenda of women, trans, or non-binary folks.

I'm writing to myself as well, since during my first years of parish ministry, I sometimes used my power wrongly and hurtfully.

I contributed to a Unitarian Universalist male ministerial culture that was misogynist and abusive.

We all know that women have been bravely and boldly joining the "Me Too" movement with regard to sexual harassment and violation. Some abused men have rightly signed on too. But I'm imploring, as we re-energize commandment #7, for brothers, of any and all stripes, to build a *Me Too* movement, wherein men sign on as violators, harassers, and perpetrators of any form of gender malfeasance. And, more than that, if we're willing to sign on as violators (in some sense, in some way, at some time), then we must also be ready and willing to sign on as repairers. We're summoned to launch a *Me Too* movement *for* gender justice.

There's another challenging area for adult men to undertake. We need to mentor boys toward manhood. The growth will prove mutual, and our entire society benefits from a wholesome boys-to-men venture. In enhancing the worth and dignity of our young boys, girls, and transgender children, we will be strengthening our earthly village.

The African maxim puts it vividly: "If our young are not initiated into the village, they will burn it down to feel the heat." Today's young boys and teenagers are often unmotivated and underachieving and turn to bullying, drugs, violence, depression, and gangs. These youngsters engage in reckless behavior as their way of proving that they aren't little boys anymore, that they are men, and that they belong to our world. But, of course, they're doing so in a misguided, futile, and destructive fashion.

A recent survey of boys in the 8th grade revealed that 90% of them see their primary goal in life as "making lots of money." And in over a million high schools, only 19% feel valued by their society.

Furthermore, every day, three boys commit suicide, higher among LGBTQ kids.

It's not just that teens have gone bad in our modern world. No, the grievous fault lays with us adult males. We need to provide them with respectful bonds and ceremonial markings, far deeper, safer, and richer than merely a first drink or first sexual encounter, garnering a driver's license, or even voting.

We need to furnish an integral portion of the scaffolding for the younger generation. We adult men need to help our adolescent boys know that with every privilege comes a corresponding responsibility. We need to companion them in transformative rites-of-passage. Our youth yearn for meaningful, heart-to heart, intergenerational exchanges such as those they receive in our *Coming-of Age* programs or in a whole host of mentoring endeavors.

Dr. Paul Kivel, founder of the *Oakland Men's Project*, puts it compellingly:

> *I imagine a world in which boys are strong and powerful but also gentle and caring, not only able to get by, but also to get ahead, even more so to get together with others to work to improve our society. And never at the expense of our daughters.*
>
> *I use two questions to gauge boy's growth: "What will our sons stand for? And who will they stand with?"*
>
> *It makes a profound difference in our actions and in the world when we say of every boy we encounter: "Here is one of my sons!"*

Most every occasion I'm with my own children and grandchildren, as well as with children and youth in our greater society, I try to engage them in meaningful conversation. Without sounding pompous or pushy, I remind each precious youngster, in one way or another, that the goal during our lifetime is to deliver, yea to be, a good gift to the world every day we're blessed to breathe.

So, please listen in and listen up, my brothers. I'm not interested in shaming my male gender but simply in calling us to full accountability. I'm calling for a transformative manifesto and behavior. Men made patriarchy possible, but that does not mean patriarchy is immutable. There remains a glimmer of hope, as Robert Jensen states in his book, *The End of Patriarchy: Radical Feminism for Men* (2017):

> *It is important to remember that patriarchy is not the default setting for human societies, but rather a recent development. In the 200,000 years of the species, homo sapiens, patriarchy accounts for less than 5% of our evolutionary history.*

With incessant vigilance and revolutionary justice, we can evolve a post-patriarchal period in human history, move by move by move by move. In the Hebrew bible, women and men are considered to be "corresponding strengths." And that condition extends to non-binary and transgender folks as well. All human siblings are summoned to be corresponding strengths in maximizing joy and justice in our one and only cosmos.

Patriarchy remains a major human obstacle, and when doggedly diminished on the road toward dismantlement, everyone is freed. Humans, plants, animals, and any and all deities will be enriched and duly rejoicing! Working as "yokefellows" (St. Paul's apt term), alongside all gender identities, to make the ideals of equality substantive exemplifies healthy and mature masculinity.

In 2025, we've barely begun to approximate the mid-19th century exhortation of Margaret Fuller, American journalist and women's rights activist: "A new manifestation is at hand, a new hour is come, when Man and Woman may regard one another as brother and sister, able both to appreciate and to prophesy to one another."

Can we look at each and every sibling and honestly say: "You and I are equally worthwhile creations. I hold you in the highest regard. Your time, your tasks, your needs, your visions, your capacities, and your identity are as significant as mine and will be treated as such in our relationship!" Can we both "appreciate and prophesy to one another," as Fuller boldly bids? And although we will never realize the end of misogyny, we can *persevere*: literally see something through to the end, not the end of the problem, but to the end of our respective lives.

Moreover, throughout my 50 plus years of doing men's soulful and prophetic work, I've employed the self-identification of *WHAAMM*: that is, "white heterosexual, Anglo, able-bodied, middle-class, male." As a full-blown elder, I currently add another A: "aging." A *whaaamm* has historically been the premier perpetrator of immense prejudice and travesty. As a member of *whaaamm*, I've been a born-and-bred carrier of unearned privilege and power and must labor daily to jettison (or certainly modify) my own condition.

Brittany Packnett Cunningham (1984-), American activist, co-founder of *Campaign Zero*, and the 2018 Ware lecturer at our UUA General Assembly, exhorts: "The more you benefit from white supremacy, the more you have to be responsible to dismantle it, every single time. You must try to be actively, intentionally, and consistently anti-racist." And I would add: be consistently anti-misogynistic and anti-xenophobic. Henceforth, until my ashes are scattered, I'm pledging, as are other self-identified males, to practice the messy, endless labor of demolishing the interwoven oppressive systems that keep us on top and whaaamming away.

As a Unitarian Universalist committed to our 16th century historical principle of *semper reformanda* ("always reforming"), I'm adding an ER on the end of whaaamm to indicate my commitment to be ever-reforming. As a whaaamm-er, I vow to incarnate a better and braver version of self and ministry, aiming to observe the razor-sharp demand of our up-to-date ministers' covenant:

To use our power constructively and with intention,
mindful of our potential unconsciously
to perpetuate systems of oppression.

To be sure, as a white male elder, my seasons are waning; nonetheless, they remain filled with faith, hope, and love. My *man*date is to be a *semper reformanda* force—internally, externally, and eternally—in order to grow a universe of mounting justice and joy.

Native American author, Catherine Attla (1927-2012), enlarges the moral horizon of respectfulness:

There's a really big law that we have to obey. That law is respect.

We have to treat everything with respect. The Earth, the animals, the plants, the sky. Everything.

"Big" because the quintessential principle of the interdependent cosmic web of existence is respect. Everything else proceeds from this moral cornerstone, and all forms of respect are interrelated. The seventh commandment dares us to bring not only races, gender identities, classes, and nations but other species within our moral circle of concern, consciousness, and connectedness. Animals and plants are not lower than humans, only different genera. We are inextricably tethered and share earth's home.

This ceremony synchronizes with the teaching attributed to Rabbi Yohanan who said:

> *"Even if the Torah had not been given, we would nonetheless have learned modesty from the cat, which covers its excrement, and that stealing is objectionable from the ant, which does not take grain from another ant, and forbidden relations from the dove, which is faithful to its partner, and proper relations from the rooster, which first appeases the hen and then mates with it."*

We humans are summoned to *behold*. "Behold the lilies of the field," as the Nazarene invited. Behold the moon. Behold the raccoon and goat. Behold the sunset. Behold even the tornado, for we cannot wrest beauty from the whole. Everywhere we roam in the universe we find loveliness mingled with the disturbing and ruthless. And behold the rocks, for a brook without rocks has no song.

Beyond affirming our *relatedness* to the entire ecosystem, beyond displaying *respect* for all living things, there exists the undeniable charge for us to be *responsible*. In the Garden of Eden story, we were given the mandate to tend it, "to till and keep it," to be caretakers. Life itself was deeded to human beings under the requirement that we remain obedient to its basic laws and, moreover, that we prove to be responsible for creation's well-being. And *tilling* implies more than possessing a green thumb. Some of us don't own green thumbs, and we're hardly exempt from the caretaking of earth. I used to plant gardens in Iowa, a land with as lush, fertile ground as anywhere in America. I learned to keep the empty seed packages, because sometimes they were about the right size for storing my puny crop! *Tilling* means nothing less than cultivating an evergreen spirit. We must be stewards, even if not successful planters.

As we gain more abiding respect for soil and sky, plants and animals, we will grow less likely to treat our fellow humans with disregard or abusively. Each individual act of compassion for the natural world, each measure of conservation, each decision against dirtying the air, land, or water ... these gifts honor "the big law." We cannot achieve the perfect outcome; we can only approximate deeds that are helpful not harmful in any given situation. As Mark Nepo (1951-), poet and spiritual advisor, writes: "Every time we meet in kindness and truth, we strengthen the immune system of the global body." Indeed, we do.

There is a unity in the ecosphere within which we exist in quivering ambivalence. We are unable to comprehend fully the whole and all its precarious rhythms and equities in the very moment in which we are required to act. We ask and answer with our very lives: "What can the planet best do through me at this particular juncture of my earthly stay?"

In these late years of our planet's need, we will most likely never halt either our intentional plundering or our accidental blundering, even the most respectful among us. Our spaceship is fragile and frail, and so are we. Yet our planet will presumably survive, no matter what earthlings do or fail to do, because the cosmos knows how to heal itself. Nonetheless, we humans can leave no greater moral or spiritual legacy after our death, than having handled the earth and all its inhabitants with exceeding thoughtfulness and responsibility.

If and when we choose to practice the big law, we can rest assured that the other commandments will be respectfully handled.

Study questions for personal reflection and/or group discussion

(1) In what ways have your sexual relationships proven to be either meaningful or hurtful in your life?

(2) What are the core behavioral aspects of mature sexuality from your perspective?

(3) How do you currently practice *fidelity* and *hesed* (steadfast kindness) at home, play, work, and in the larger world?

(4) In what ways have you been prone to adulterate or diminish your relational bonds?

(5) Enumerate some defining qualities of a healthy partnership or friendship.

(6) Describe situations when you have been perceived and/or treated as a stranger, outsider, or alien.

(7) What does it mean for all human beings to be respected as "corresponding strengths"?

(8) Share your feelings and thoughts about patriarchy or toxic masculinity.

(9) What role does the *Big Law* of *respect* play in your daily relations with humans, animals, and plants?

Chapter VIII

Robbery Diminishes Everybody

VIII. Thou shall not steal
—Exodus 20:15

*I vow not to take what is not given,
but to be satisfied with what I have.*
—Second of the 10 Grave Buddhist Precepts

*We are all guests with limited reservations, so don't
pillage the resources, insult the natives,
or steal the towels; instead, be hospitable.*
—Rev. John Taylor

This commandment insists that property is a kind of extension of the owner's self. Therefore, acts of theft, cheating, conning, defrauding, and swindling are violations of personhood. Robbery assaults our very humanity. It's a perennial problem in today's world, with property thievery occurring in some form every three seconds. And then there's the gross uptick in identity theft. I suffered from a "data breach" just recently. Furthermore, greed and materialism are rife in our American culture. And we dare not forget workers who are not fairly compensated for their labor or receive inadequate wages.

That's why, on a communal scale, mature morality requires us to construct economic and social systems wherein everybody can dwell equitably in life, liberty, and the pursuit of happiness. What follows is a poignant story of yesteryear illustrating this truth. The city of Toledo had a mayor called "Golden Rule Jones." Once in a while, Jones went down to preside at the police court. On a winter day, during the Depression of the 1930's, the police brought in someone charged with stealing groceries. The individual pleaded guilty and offered no excuse except that he had no money and no job.

"I've got to fine you," said Mayor Jones. "You stole, not from the community responsible for these conditions but from a particular person. So I fine you ten dollars." But then the mayor reached into his own pocket, pulled out a bill, and said, "Here's the money to pay your fine." Then he picked up his hat and handed it to the bailiff. "Now, I'm going to fine everybody in this courtroom fifty cents, or as much thereof as you happen to have with you, for living in a town where a person has to steal groceries in order to eat. Bailiff, please go through the courtroom and collect the fines and give them to the defendant."

Or, as biblical wisdom (Luke 12:48) exhorts: "To whom much is given, much will be required …" If we have been blessed with talents, wealth, knowledge, time, and the like, it's expected that we share said gifts to benefit others.

Slavery is another dreadful form of robbery. The birth of the Decalogue occurs in direct response to the Israelites being freed from slavery in Egypt. Therefore, this commandment outlaws any form of "taking people" or bondage. The entire slavery system in our New World, rightly termed "America's original sin," is roundly condemned in #8. Howard Zinn (1922-2010), American historian, socialist intellectual, and World War II veteran, warned: "Racism is not just about hurting others but also about taking, stealing, and blocking good things."

Reparations are due for African Americans and Native Americans as well as for Mexicans, from whom my home state California and much of the Southwest were essentially stolen. People who have been robbed should be paid back, plain and simple. Moreover, in our contemporary society, the blatant and devious modes of slavery and servitude are legion and spreading.

And then there's rape: to steal, seize, or carry away by force. Radical feminist Andrea Dworkin contextualizes this horrific exploitation:

> *In the Old Testament, marriage laws protected the father's ownership of the daughter. Any early strictures against rape were strictures against robbery—against the theft of property. Women belonged to men; the laws of marriage sanctified that ownership; rape was the theft of a woman from her owner. The biblical laws are the basis of the social order and to this day have not been repudiated.*

This 8th commandment summons us to honor and care for the weakest and most oppressed members of humanity ... the last, the least, and the lost among us. It exemplifies respectfulness for every human being. After all, justice means making sure that a fair and sufficient amount of everything that belongs to people gets to them and stays with them: be it food, job security, freedom, health care, housing, or dignity.

Radical Protestant theologian and long-time justice-maker, William Sloane Coffin (1924-2006), underscored the heart of our human struggle:

> *Am I my neighbor's keeper? No, I am my neighbor's neighbor. Human unity is not something we are called upon to create, only to recognize.*
>
> *Homelessness is devastating, suggesting neither comfort nor companionship, dignity nor grace, and precious little identity.*
>
> *To have no place is to be no place.*

One of the just and kind covenants we exhibit at our Uptown Homeless Center is having clients, in appropriate situations, serve the Center in return. Hence, you will observe regulars sweeping the patio, lugging crates of food, cleaning the bathroom, sorting clothes, or assisting newer folks in navigating the tricky passage toward possibly garnering shelter or work—helping fellow homeless take an exit off the highway from drugs, violence, or poverty.

One morning, Clyde came to our desk and said: "I believe in reciprocity" and proceeded to sing-song out each letter of the word: "R-E-C-I-P-R-O-C-I-T-Y. You gave me some food and clothing yesterday. What's there for me to do at the Center today? It's my turn to help others!" Most of our volunteers are elders and crones with bad knees and balky backs, so we welcomed Clyde to do some "heavy lifting" around the Center. He thanked us for the privilege of being a reciprocal partner at Uptown. Since that pivotal moment,

Clyde has returned, both for services *and* opportunities to serve.

Here's the example of another service-partner. Arthur walked into our Uptown Center, looking morose and sounding downtrodden, clearly out of sorts. He said: "I'm tired and worn-out. I asked God to take me home soon, but he hasn't called yet. Suicide isn't an option, since God saved me awhile back, and if I destroy myself, I'll harm God. I won't do it; so I just keep waiting around for God's call to come!" We got to bantering back and forth, and I noticed that Arthur was carrying a small guitar on his back. I told him that I played some too and offered the following invitation: "Arthur, it's kind of humdrum around the Center right now; why don't you serenade us with one of your favorite songs?"

So, Arthur pulled out his scuffed and worn, pawn-shop special and strummed the Eagles' classic song, "Hotel California" (1977), vaguely familiar to me. Arthur's raw rendition was so stirring, I told him that I planned to listen to it again on YouTube, then, after learning and chording it, incorporate "Hotel California" into my own inventory of songs. "Thank you, Arthur, for delivering such an inspirational gift to all of us at Uptown, today!"

Arthur wasn't done, asking me if I might duet with him sometime in a nearby park. I was caught off-guard yet proceeded to skirt Arthur's request by telling him that I would rather bring my guitar someday to the Center, and we might play together there.

You see, there's an unwritten yet appropriate "rule of boundaries" in social service: you don't mingle off-site with clients. You don't go out to lunch together, and they aren't invited to your home for an evening visit. The fact is that not all strangers can become friends in our lives. Nonetheless, the inner spirits of Arthur and Tom connected that day, and maybe there will be more meaningful associations along our mutual paths. My heart certainly remains open to our crooning "Hotel California" together ... at the Center.

Lo and behold, years later, I now sing weekly in the courtyard at our new Center, so Arthur's spark ignited a musical flame in my soul. I sit in a corner of the St. Luke's refugee church patio while clients are receiving food and clothing, taking showers, participating in recovery programs, and garnering counsel. I sing familiar and uplifting ballads. I'm not an entertainer, so much as a "singing companion." And, once in a while, service-partners sing, strum, or chat with me.

Recently, Millie came over and timidly requested: "Can I just sing something of my own and have you riff along on the guitar?" She continued: "You know, out on the streets, it gets terribly lonely, and I've been talking a lot to myself—even composing some poems and songs—to keep my spirits up. And here's a song, Tom, I'd like to share with you!" And Millie's gift of song brought some solace to both of our souls as well as to nearby Uptowners. No one's homelessness was cured that morning, but a measure of companionship and comfort was delivered. Remember, we humans are servants not saviors. And I've rarely met a human being who doesn't personally prosper when either serving or being served. Compassionate behavior enhances rather than robs us of our selfhood ... giver and receiver alike.

The venerated hymn titled *There's a Wideness in God's Mercy* reminds us that those who live on the outskirts of human favor—especially the foreigner, the destitute, and the pariah—are lovingly cradled. Being created in God's image, every last one of us possesses the capacity to embrace and be embraced. I resonate with the way that Jonathan Sacks (1948-2020), chief rabbi of the United

Kingdom and the Commonwealth of Nations from 1991-2013, phrased it:

> *What makes the first chapter of Genesis revolutionary is its statement that every human being, regardless of class, color, culture, or creed is in the image and likeness of God. In the ancient world it was rulers, kings, emperors, and pharaohs who were held to be in the image of God. What Genesis was saying is that we are all royalty. We each have equal dignity in the kingdom of faith under the sovereignty of God.*

At our best, we earthlings are trying to build a "*dignitarian world*" as one associate describes it, and to do so, we must regard one another as "service-partners." Shirley Chisholm (1924-2005), an American politician from New York, who, in 1968, became the first black woman ever to be elected to the United States Congress, tendered this moral statement: "Service is the rent we pay for the privilege of being here on earth!" Every day, you and I are summoned to pay a portion of our earthly rent.

At our same Homeless Center, one of our regular "rent-payers" has her 10-year-old daughter "volunteer" with her, on off-days from Olivia's school. Her parents feel that serving others is integral to their daughter's upbringing and "life-curriculum." As they soulfully phrase it: "We want Olivia to start learning how to give back in her early years, so that she might later on major in compassion!"

Olivia's prime joy is making lemonade, selling it on the street outside our Center, and then contributing any earned money to support Uptown. Olivia is a full-fledged teammate on our crew, taking the time to talk with clients, sweeping the courtyard, and getting the showers ready. She does it all; she gives her all. Olivia has chosen the pathway of servanthood. She is living with humane eyes and attentive hands. And, lo and behold, this past Monday, I learned that Olivia had "recruited" her local grandmother to volunteer. Love is spreading and multiplying at our homeless center, thanks, in part, to a caring pre-teenager named Olivia.

Down-deep, every human wishes to be fairer and kinder toward self and others. We're all in this pain-soaked life-and-death excursion together. Kindness enables us to exemplify our bedrock kinship. And there's never a wrong time or way to be kind.

Stealing refers to subtle and offhanded manifestations of greed, exploitation, and embezzlement. It means taking what isn't ours or isn't given to us. Beware of the ways when you and might casually violate this commandment. In addition to issues of economic and social justice, #8 prompts us to halt the spiritual, intellectual, and emotional robberies, of both property and personhood, we commit. There exist rampant non-material thefts of time, of ideas, of space, and even of one another's qualities such as joy and assurance. Our daughter is currently pursuing a post-graduate degree, in her early fifties, in combating cybercrime (criminal activities perpetrated by usage of computers or the internet), focusing upon sex trafficking with children via the "dark web." We must monitor and minimize the pillage and theft we commit, both intentionally and unintentionally, in all zones of our lives. When robbery of any form occurs, trust is eroded, and the worthiness of both victim and perpetrator is assaulted. Humanity suffers.

And, friends, another form of robbery is shown in the failure to utilize our God-given talents. We currently outsource our creativity and memory to technology such as smartphones. Our mental capacity shrinks as we succumb increasingly to the skill set of Google. We're committing what I call "self-stealing." We're robbing ourselves and, therewith, the greater world. Bob Moawad, a prominent inspirational speaker, alleges: "You can't leave footprints in the sands of time, if you're sitting on your butt, and who wants to leave butt prints in the sands of time?" In refined religious terms, such behavior, or lack thereof, is termed *slothfulness.*

We combat slothfulness by incarnating our healthiest desires. Biblically put: "Whatsoever thy hand findest to do, do it with thy *might.*" (Ecclesiastes 9:10) We utilize all of our inherent might precisely where we're planted. Before making a case for sloth as a deadly sin, perhaps the sneakiest of them all, it should be noted that the sloth as an animal exhibits useful habits and traits, according to both scientists and lay observers.

First, immobility is a virtue for sloths. Stillness is their best defense, making them harder to see. Housed in the crotch of a tree, arms folded across its chest, the sloth resembles a bunch of dead leaves. The sloth reminds humans that there's a proper time to be immobile and disguised during the course of our lives. The sloth honors the Sabbath (the 4th commandment) in its own matchless manner.

Second, the sloth is a generous and accommodating animal for a vast group of specialized insects living in its hair. Sloths harbor moths, beetles, ticks as well as other assorted mites, and they receive frequent visits from itinerant mosquitoes and flies. Would that we humans were such obliging hosts? A bit of radical hospitality goes a long way, doesn't it?

Third, the sloth is an excellent swimmer; the gut gives it extra buoyancy. That fits some of us, too.

Fourth, sloths mate while hanging from a branch. I won't attempt any comparisons on that habit.

Finally, sloths avoid putting excessive pressure on any single species by exploiting a wide variety of trees. They have, in effect, adapted harmoniously to their environment. Would that we humans could say the same! So, as you can see, these masters of digestion, champions of sleep, and gurus of the pendulous, loafing life have much to recommend themselves. Moving from this portrait of the sloth as an animal, let's look at sloth as a sin.

In the Middle Ages, catholic leaders listed seven deadly sins which, I guess, they thought to be the most interesting and original of our human blunders. Their catalogue fits modern society quite snugly: pride, covetousness, gluttony, lust, wrath, envy, and sloth are still periodic roadblocks to self-care growth and are referenced subtly in our wrestling with the Ten Commandments.

When you peruse this log of sins, you wonder how sloth ever slithered into such salacious company. I'm not sure why sloth was canonized, as it were, to be a deadly sin, but I harbor strong hunches. Sloth is a sin, because it gives rise to torpor of mind and sluggishness of conscience. Sloth perpetrates robbery; it steals humans from wielding our innate and blessed capacities.

A quick glance at biblical history reveals something startling. We like to characterize biblical sinners as individuals with overweening pride. It was, in fact, their timidity and cowardice that let the sly serpent seduce them into a state of slothfulness. And beware, right now, you and I can, without batting an eyelash, grow emotionally stale, intellectually stymied, and spiritually blocked—in short, moribund, while breathing. As American political journalist and world peace advocate, Norman Cousins (1915-1990) wrote: "The real tragedy in life is what dies inside us while we are still alive."

Sloth is a sin of omission, a sin of neglect, a sin of self-robbery. We avoid the very thing we can or ought to do. We were formed by the Creator to be change-agents rather than ineffectual bystanders. We were born to make a difference, however modest, during our stay on earth. Consequently, when the proverbial judgment day comes, we'll be asked: "Did you participate in the moral struggles of your place and time?" Sloths will answer: "Well, I just never quite got around to it!" Servants will say: "I showed up and delivered my best!"

Doing what we can, with what we possess, and where we're located is our holy mission. Your something and my something add up to somethings, often mighty and formidable. Instead of trying to move mountains, let's start by shoveling dirt around. Rather than accomplishing one great deed, let's be willing to perform a few decent acts along the way. As the hymn of my childhood counseled: "Brighten the corner where you are!"

St. Paul wrote: "Let your steps by guided by such light as you have." None of us possess all the light we truly need: light as spark, light as truth, and light as warmth. However, we each boast a measure of beam and glow in our souls. So, instead of waiting around for magical bursts of light from beyond, let's employ the blaze that is already within. We have untapped capacity to brighten our days, radiate energy, and guide our very life-steps. We'll be pleasantly startled whenever we turn on our inner lights, and so will our neighbors.

Perhaps, most importantly, Commandment #8 reminds us that the possessive instinct has its limits. There are realities which cannot be owned, only enjoyed. We need to use things and relate to people rather than the other way around.

Humans, plants, and animals are uniformly guests on the soil of this magnificent universe. As Alistair Shearer (1947-), a cultural historian specializing in the art and architecture of the Indian sub-continent, eloquently testifies:

In truth, everything arises in order to disappear.
Everything we have, everything we think we are,
must at some point be surrendered, for it is only
on loan from the bounty of the Divine.

So many wonders of nature and humanity cannot be possessed. Like love and stars, exuberance and oceans.

There's more. As we amble homeward, may we pay off our debts (relational as well as financial ones), leaving life as current and connected as possible. And for goodness sake, let's not wait until our death-bed to be robbed of the chance to speak our truths, heal our conflicts, shed our paraphernalia, and tender our goodbyes.

I heartily endorse the sentiment of Paul in Romans 13:8:

Owe no one anything, except to love one another.

As we seniors approach our date with death, tapering everything we have and hold down to love itself is a consummate discipline. We're roused to plow meticulously through our closets, cupboards, files, accounts, and odds and ends. We can take our time, if we're still cogent and in charge. To whom might we owe money, a conciliatory word, clothes, a photograph, crystal, or miscellaneous artifacts? Perhaps we owe an overdue embrace or a moldy, yet meaningful, book. If so, whenever doable, I prod us to deliver, any of the above, personally.

And how about owing a word of hope? Surely, as we amble down our closing laps of existence, we dare not forget to be hope-filled creatures. Hope is trusting in spite of the evidence and watching the evidence change ... no, *helping* the evidence change via our own behavior. Hope is the dynamic of history and the energy of transformation. Every morning, until our dying day, we want to embody a full dose of hopefulness; we want to make sure that we choose the team of hopers rather than the squad of disparagers. Hopers unite!

Progressives have consciously thrown our lot with an unrelentingly hopeful faith, and by hope I'm not referring to optimism. The optimist tends to be fanciful and dreamy-eyed, often leaving the world's problems up to Jorge or God, Georgette or Goddess to solve while remaining a bouncy, mindless cheer-leader on the sidelines. The optimist resembles the person who gazes at the stars but is perennially at the mercy of the puddles in the road.

Instead, the hoper isn't convinced that something will happen but is willing to work their rear off to make sure that something good might just come to be ... even if but partially or gradually. The optimist lays back; the hoper moves forward. The hoper is an activated human being, one who arouses in self and others a passion for the possible. Hopers stay on purpose, even when not immediately successful.

I wasn't surprised, the other day, when I discovered that the words *hope* and *hop* come from the same root, one that means "to leap up in expectation." Isn't that how it feels to be hopeful—a palpable eagerness for what is to come? When I'm hopping, I'm a real hoper, and conversely, when I hope, I'm likely to be hopping about ... even in my hoary years!

We humans add to the universe, even as we are created and sustained by it. Being connected to all of life, hopers—as Unitarian

Universalist Dr. Bernard Loomer emphasized in his relational theology—are charged "to heal and strengthen that part of the cosmic web where we nest."

"Attention, attention, attention," wrote Zen master Ikkyu centuries ago when asked to capture the highest wisdom. "But what does attention mean?" pressed his questioner. Master Ikkyu replied, "Well, attention means attention!"

The etymology of attention comes from the Latin *attendere*, meaning to "stretch." One way or another, in authentic living, our spirits are painstakingly stretched. Our hearts and minds, bodies and consciences are stretched as well.

Hopers are stretchers. Finishing life well means daily stretching *upward* to the sky, *downward* to the earth, *backward* in remembrance, *outward* in compassion, and *onward* toward unfathomable tomorrows. Stretching ... then stretching some more. Which is what I'm doing right now, taking a breather from my writing.

The saints of yesteryear used to aver *solvitur ambulando* or "it is solved by walking." But the time may well arrive when we are physically hobbled, wheel-chair bound, or bed-ridden, and we can't walk. Nonetheless, our spirits can keep circumambulating: hopping and hoping homeward in reasonable fashion. The hoper differs from the pessimist as well as the optimist. Realism would often demand pessimism. But the hopeful person talks not in terms of crisis, a concept that usually overwhelms and immobilizes us, but in terms of issues and challenges and jobs ... with our names on some of them. Everything grows manageable when reduced to doable tasks. Remember hope arouses passion for the possible.

The pessimist says: "Blessed are they who believe in nothing, for they shan't be disappointed!" Hopers, on the contrary, agree with that portion of the *Desiderata* that says: "Whatever your labors and aspirations in the noisy confusion of life, keep peace with your soul. With all its shame, drudgery, and broken dreams, it's still a beautiful world." Indeed, it is.

Hopers know that the best anti-depressant available on the market involves movement of mouth, movement of body, movement of conscience, movement of heart ... serving the larger world in specific, loving deeds ... until we enter our graves.

Cynicism is all around us; in fact, in the past few years, a new sort of "progressive" cynicism, if you will, has arisen. Progressive cynics harbor the viewpoint that Western culture and American society are hopelessly oppressive. I would agree that contemporary culture is drenched in racism, sexism, homophobia and a whole array of interlinking persecutions. But we reformists believe that cynicism is spiritual treason. We assert that no problem in human relations is truly insoluble. We may never solve it in our lifetimes, but we refuse to quit on justice, quit on joy, quit on mercy, and quit on civilization. We keep on keeping on, because we're incurable hopers! It's downright crucial for each of us, in our own ways, all of our days and nights, to go on record as opposing evil. Of course, it's important to be effective in halting some of the proliferating injustices in society, but if we can't stop them, then, at least we must *oppose* them.

As author Barbara Kingsolver puts it: "The very least we can do in our life is to figure out what we hope for. And the most we can do is live inside that hope." Our job is to enlist as sentinels who never stop singing and serving.

Our ultimate earthly aim: reckon up and leave life ... debt-free, up-to-date, and kindness-filled. Every moment of my life I ask myself: what is the most loving thing for me to say, be, do right now? As a bona fide elder, I'm keenly aware that my remaining moments are dear. I pay close attention to insuring that they aren't lost, misspent, or stolen ... by the passage of time itself, other pilgrims, or by my own carelessness.

Most of all, in wrangling honorably with these Ten Commandments, we're urged to depart life in gratitude. I concur with the sentiment of author Annie Dillard (1945-): "Say thank you, rather than please, when facing death ... as a guest thanks a host at the door." There's a time and place to beg and barter during the tattered course of our lives. It's a natural part of our human make-up to whine and plead, but death is the occasion, is it not, to burst forth in sheer thankfulness for a life unexpected?

As first century Roman statesperson, Cicero, put it: "Gratitude is not only the greatest of virtues, but the parent of all the others." For when we're grateful, we're able to initiate the full life, ready to exude gladness and pursue justice, and eager to grow compassion and bathe in serenity.

In a Pogo episode, Churchy LaFemme sits wailing in the back of the rowboat after seeing a newspaper headline: "Sun Will Burn Out in Three Billion Years, Killing All Life!" Churchy cries: "Woe is me; I'm too young to die." Porky reprimands him, saying, "Shut up, you're lucky to be here in the first place!" And so we are. Lucky to be here in the first place!

You know, the mathematical odds of our being born are something like one in 700 trillion. No two snowflakes are alike; no two humans are the same either. Even identical twins differ. It's a marvel that each of us, irrepeatables, walks the earth at this twinkling in time. Never allow that truth to be swiped from your consciousness.

In *Cat's Cradle*, a fanciful science-fiction novel, Kurt Vonnegut (1922-2007) conveys this same attitude through the Bokonist Death ritual. The Bokonists, you see, serve God by lying down on the floor, raising their legs, and massaging each other's feet, sole to sole, while communing with God. When one of the old Bokonists is about to die, she recites the prayer, "God made mud. I was some of the mud that got to suit up and look around. What memories for mud to have. I loved everything I saw. Lucky me, lucky mud!" If we're bold enough to wear this attitude all the way until our death, then like the Bokonists, when the time comes to release our consciousness back to the greater planetary pool, we can bellow: "How blessed I was to live—lucky me, lucky mud!"

None of us asks to be born. There's no special merit involved with our singular arrivals. We didn't earn the privilege of life. We were lucky. Whether we look at existence scientifically or religiously or both, it's an unspeakable miracle, a wonder, a gift of grace that we exist.

Every morning I arise, I take a deep breath and shout forth: "Wow, it's good to be alive. I'm downright lucky to be here. I'm taking nothing for granted. I'm going full-bore today!" Well, at my age, I don't spring out of bed anymore. I usually crawl or stumble out, straightway to the bathroom, but, nonetheless, thankful for the gift of yet another unmerited 24 hours. Being grateful energizes, enhances, and elevates our very being, from start to finish.

Let me relate the story of how gratitude and I first joined forces. It was a clumsy start. My parents were worried about me as a toddler, because I didn't seem willing or able to muster detectable words until about five or so.

Yet once I started to talk, albeit late, I emerged in sentences ...

and look at me now, words have become my trade.

When I first started to talk, I remember my Mom pulling me aside and saying: "Tommy, before you get going, I've a few tips to offer. Son, there exist words that heal and words that hurt, and I want you to major in the first kind."

Secondly, my sweetheart, there are five phrases, that I hope will be liberally sprinkled throughout the course of your life. They aren't complicated or fancy. They don't belong to scholars or gurus. They belong to everyone. They're words, my precious, that mend, that soothe, and that give life! So, I pass them on for your safe keeping and caring use. And, whenever you're not sure what to say, either be quiet or offer one of the following modest phrases: "Thank you. I love you. How are you? I'm sorry. Tell me more."

Mom continued: "Now, of course, there are going to be inappropriate times to use any of these words. But, almost universally, Tommy, these phrases express gratitude, respect, and love—the most important freight any language can ever carry." But of all five phrases Mom passed on to me, her clear favorite was "thank you!" which, she quickly added, came with two conditions. First, "if you never share your gratitude, son, it won't reach its destination. Plus, if you don't offer thanks when you feel it, you won't get around to doing it later. The moment will pass. So, gratitude is basic, Tommy. It's life's spiritual engine; all the big virtues are motored by gratitude. Indeed, everything of worth flows from a thankful heart!" That was the main lecture of my entire growing up. And I've spent the rest of my years trying to live up to it.

Whether arguing or rejoicing, the thankful person remains thankful. Whether celebrating beauty or protesting injustice, the thankful person remains thankful. Whether laughing or crying, fearful or in pain, the thankful person remains thankful. Thanksgiving isn't a passing state or an annual feast. It's a perpetual condition of the religious pilgrim. Thankful ... even amidst the trying season of death.

Dear ones, every love relationship ends in a loss: departure, divorce, or death. My treasured 50+ years with my life-mate, Carolyn, physically ended during the very months when I was writing this book. Sadly, she died without getting to offer her brilliant and unflinching critique of it. Every moment we share with loved ones is precious and fleeting. Everything and everyone are *impermanent* as the Buddhists remind. Consequently, we're summoned to cherish each hello and goodbye ... in preparation for the final farewell. We need to keep our loves and friendships clean, up-to-date, and kindhearted.

Carolyn and I were yoked as teammates and soul mates. We aspired to share, as equals, every aspect of our respective journeys. I'm sorely missing the constant touches of our blemished hands, the poignant talks and languorous walks, our singing together (wow, what a natural harmonizer Carolyn was), even our squabbles and holes, and we had them. Blessedly, we were current with our regrets and forgiveness when she died in our family room. We vowed to support the flourishing of our partner's future, when we ourselves were no longer alive.

The closing days of Carolyn's life were a spiritual summation to a wondrous journey. To be sure, they were filled with shock, anguish, and gaffes, but essentially, her existence was completed in the attentive and intimate presence of her family. She got to come home to go home, soaking in three generations of abiding affection! I was sleeping in the bed next to Carolyn, holding her hand or massaging her body, singing songs such as *Love Will Guide Us* or *I've Got Peace Like a River* ... and letting her know, amidst her increasing fog, that she could surrender and return to the Eternal Light and Love from whence she came. We initially met and fell in love singing, and I wanted to sing her on her way. I'm more mystical than Carolyn, but we held in common the Universalist gospel of *Everlasting Love*.

So, I would keep chanting in her ear: "There is a love holding me; there is a love holding you; there is a love holding all ... we rest in this love." Yes, we ultimately return to the embrace of Divine Love.

I'm currently wobbling, hither and yon, and I'll keep on grieving the remainder of my days and nights, but I'm also soaking in gratitude. My therapist charges me to "live dualistically": cherishing the past while charting the future. A colleague calls it "thanks-grieving." And, fortunately, right now, gratitude is holding serve. I'm grateful that Carolyn and I gambled all we had on our partnership ... grateful that we lived heart to heart, from start to finish, and that her fingerprints are all over me.

Tenderly and thankfully, onward I go ... meandering in new country, aspiring to grow beyond what I'll never get over.

Study questions for personal reflection and/or group discussion

(1) Describe some of the ways in which you have committed various forms of robbery, either overtly or unknowingly?

(2) Share your thoughts and feelings about "America's original sin" or the slavery system as practiced in the United States ... from 1619 forward?

(3) In what ways have you had to battle slothfulness in your journey?

(4) In your own fashion, how do you try to build a "dignitarian world" or "pay your rent for the privilege of being here on earth?"

(5) Delineate the boundaries of what is and what is not yours. What truly belongs to you? Your body (address the issue of reproductive rights) as a male, female, trans or non-binary person, your memories, your material goods. your decisions, your time, etc.? Share your notes, with loved ones and friends, if you wish.

(6) Realizing the illusion of ultimate *ownership*, you still are summoned to be a steward of your whole earthly existence. How are you aspiring to be a good steward of your time, talents, and treasures?

(7) As you inevitably age, what possessions are you shedding and which ones do you wish to retain? And how are you saying farewell to your dreams and capacities, animosities and attachments? Are you reasonably up-to-date and debt-free?

(8) Share examples of how gratitude has been displayed during the course of your journey thus far.

Chapter IX

Seek, Find, Face, Tell, and Do the Truth

IX. Thou shall not bear false witness against your neighbor
—Exodus 20:16

*Speak the truth, each one to our neighbor,
because we are members of one another.*
—Ephesians 4:25

*Being truthful isn't just about what we say.
It's about how we move in the world, how we are.
Truthfulness means making a straight line
from our convictions to what we say and to what we do.
It is an act of love, act of resistance, an act of courage.*
—Rev. Dr. Jacqui Lewis

This commandment, although referring to the judicial system, upholds integrity in every area of our lives. Few of us are outright murderers or thieves but, I dare conjecture, all of us are conveyers of lies. While absolute honesty may not always be the best policy, we need to monitor our proclivities to gossip, stereotype, perpetuate falsehoods and smokescreens, slander, exaggerate, or peddle little *white* lies ... all forms of what Rabbi Rachel S. Mikva sagely terms: "weapons of the mouth." Sadly, our current American political landscape is currently strewn with fake news and conspiracy theories.

Note that this commandment, unlike any of the other nine, refers to our "neighbor," implying that our untruths not only impact our family or friends but also affect the greater society. We need to protect and advance our *neighborhood* as a whole, both in word and deed.

Before we delineate the ways of truthfulness, the ninth commandment charges us to address lying. "To lie is to intentionally mislead others when they expect honest communication." Lies, slowly but surely, can erode trust, even destroy our cherished bonds. The Talmud (*Arachin* 15b) reminds us that harmful speech damages three people: the one who is speaking; the one spoken about; and the one who is listening.

Clearly, most of us don't tell the unembellished truth, all the time. We hem and haw when asked how "we're feeling today?" or obfuscate some, to maintain privacy, when asked "how did a family member die?" There are also moments when words would prove hurtful; so silence is often the better part of valor. Furthermore, as a budding magician, I've learned verbally how to *mis*-direct and bamboozle folks all in the name of fun. And frivolous chatter and impish banter can be gifts, as long as they don't injure anyone. The key, to all Ten Commandments, sticks: "Do no harm."

But lying still occurs, at a staggering level, in today's world, according to Sam Harris, in his provocative volume (2013) on *Lying*:

> ... *one study suggests that 10% of communication between spouses is deceptive and that 38% of encounters among college students contain lies. Lying is ubiquitous. Honest people are rare and a refuge. Honesty is a gift. The benefits of telling the truth (being brutally but pragmatically honest) far outweigh the cost of lies—to yourself, to others, and to society.*

So, commandment #9 remains a germane challenge for contemporary life. At the least, it presses us to cease, or certainly minimize, "bearing false witness" against anyone whom we meet along life's pathway.

Our intention is uprightness, trying to bring our words and actions into moral alignment, so the world might be a healthier and holier place for our having spoken and behaved. Christianity strikes a golden mean between wholehearted truthfulness and destructive duplicity, when it exhorts us "to speak the truth in love." (Ephesians 4:15) Truth has countless avenues, but it yearns to be offered in a spirit of gentleness and compassion. Speaking the truth in love *is* the consummate mission of all relational bonds.

But in practice, the lines are fine, aren't they? And there are lies of both commission and omission. We dwell in the gray zones and always will. Let's move from the messiness of lying to reflections on the art of truthfulness. There's understandably much to parse.

First off, all truths are nuanced, for as Danish physicist, Niels Bohr (1865-1962), noted: "the opposite of a great truth is another truth." Hence, an open-minded religion is bristling with paradoxes, multiple truths that supplement and sharpen each other: God-fearing humanists and skeptical believers, to name but two. Responsible freedom is yet another worthwhile oxymoron. Freedom furnishes the means to pursue our bedrock human purpose: the intentional building of the beloved community on earth. But freedom *per se* doesn't necessarily get us there. It often takes us on wild goose chases or lures us into blind alleys. Freedom is the condition, not the substance, of truth. Being responsibly free is our goal. As Martin Buber (1878-1965), eminent Austrian Jewish and Israeli philosopher, claimed: "Freedom is the run before the jump, the tuning of the violin, the possibility of community. Independence is a foot-bridge, not a dwelling-place."

Consequently, our historic UUA Principles declare allegiance to a "free and *responsible* search for truth and meaning." Ours is an accountable and responsive faith that draws from the "Jewish and Christian teachings which call us to *respond* to God's love by loving our neighbors as ourselves." The cardinal truth of progressive religion is not that we are free, autonomous creatures but that we have been created for intimacy, for linking with others, for bonds. To be free *from* slaveries of all kinds is essential, but to be free *for* community is the mark of maturation.

Secondly, we recognize that truth arrives in various modes. There's no single passageway to God or supreme wisdom; rather there exist numerous, equally enlightening, avenues. For example, Unitarian Joseph Priestly, the discoverer of oxygen, came by his truths via the scientific method, a thoroughgoing empiricism. William Ellery Channing claimed reason rather than revelation as the instrumental source of his theology. Margaret Fuller, as a transcendentalist, declared that intuition was her entrée to the divine. And Dorothea Dix found her religion verified in compassion or prophetic duty. Therefore, we have historical roots and support as religious liberals for being scientists, rationalists, mystics, and activists or any conceivable blend you might select. I personally happen to be a cheerful, theological hybrid.

Pluralism triumphs in our tribe. We're called to live well with our own pursuit of the holy without belittling the routes of our siblings, be they inside or outside our chosen fold.

Thirdly, "truth," wrote Universalist forebear, Clinton Lee Scott "comes to earth in small installments." Or as another colleague once told me: "What you're saying, Tom, may well be a solid, 100% half-truth!" So often that's the case, isn't it? We race off, feeling satisfied, even smug, about some hard-earned insight, only to learn that there are many trustworthy views on the same issue and what we're fiercely clutching as final is but a partial verity.

Alas, you and I are prone to fall in love with a toe, an earlobe, or an elbow. We're captivated with parts rather than being open to the whole experience, the whole person, the whole truth. Or someone says something and it sounds reasonable, so we believe it, hook, line, and sinker. And before you know it, it becomes our "holy truth." Anyone who thinks they need to *defend* the truth isn't living from truth but from dogma. Some even believe they can kill in the name of their truth or their deity.

The damage that's been done to humans in the name of religion is staggering and abominable. A little girl and her father were talking about the some 200 denominations in this land alone, and the ten-year old daughter said: "Daddy, which *abomination* do we belong to?" Therefore, in a responsibly free religion, we possess no absolute standard of measuring THE truth. Instead we ask each person to share her/his/their own truths, and the only limitations we insist on are those necessary to preserve the greatest liberty and respect for us all. Candid and considerate conversation, not conversion, is the discipline we choose to practice. May we honor journalist Brenda Ueland's (1891-1985) two guidelines, as we unpack the Ten Commandments: "no lies and no cruelty."

Fourth, there's no shame in admitting our mistakes or even changing gears in midstream. Mahatma Gandhi once led a protest march in which many thousands of people left their jobs and homes to endure great hardship. As the march was well underway, Gandhi called a halt and disbanded it. His lieutenants came to him and said: "Mahatma, you can't do this; our march has been planned for a long time, and there are too many people involved." Gandhi's retort was, "My friends, my commitment is to truth as I see it each day, not to consistency!"

The open mind is a clogged mind, if it never changes. Whenever we "settle" in life, we ossify and turn, like Lot's wife, into useless pillars of salt. Freethinkers are re-thinkers, neither afraid to take sides nor reluctant to alter sides.

Ralph Waldo Emerson (1803-1882) was a preacher for a short spell, before he left the ministry for writing and lecturing. Among other things, the priestly and pastoral portfolios didn't appeal to him, so Emerson abandoned his initial vocation for a better fit. However, near the end of his active literary career, Emerson did some circuit riding. He would preach at various congregations, employing some of his old sermons. Waldo would come to a certain part of the homily and pensively remark: "Well, I don't believe that anymore," scratching out the given text. Then he would propose a current amendment. As Emerson summarized in his central essay, *Self-Reliance*: "a foolish consistency is the hobgoblin of little minds …"

In our quest for truth, we must be willing to revise earlier insights. This isn't readily accomplished, for it requires bravery to say farewell to intellectual offspring of yore. Paying attention to variant perspectives means pondering afresh rather than either posturing or pontificating. That's precisely what we're doing in this book, as we engage and interpret the Ten Commandments anew. We're unlocking our minds, listening deeply, and advancing up-to-date perspectives and behaviors. We're risking moral and spiritual growth.

When Michelangelo (1475-1564) painted the Sistine Chapel, he included both the major and minor prophets from the Jewish heritage. How can you tell them apart? Though cherubim appear at the ears of all, only the major prophets are listening. Oh, the unspeakable gift of paying attention and staying in dialogue, wherein our delights are multiplied and our burdens reduced. Without authentic dialogue, friends and lovers are smoldering kegs of dynamite. In dialoguing, we are, as the poet Adrienne Rich stated, "trying to extend the possibilities of truth between us." Nonetheless, dialogue can be fleeting or frustrating unless sustained by human sweat.

I've found in interpersonal relations, especially when any conversation reaches a tricky passage, even an impasse—that there exist no more golden words to open up the soul of another than plainly to inquire: "Tell me more." No amplification is needed, just the invitation: "Tell me more." In true dialogue, we may seek to convince the other of our position but, more importantly, we entertain the possibility of being persuaded by them. We pay attention and entertain constructive compromises. After all, as my friend puts it: being always right is the booby prize; creating and sustaining healthy bonds is our overriding objective.

Compromise is the trademark of the human species and a

source of adaptability in our evolution. Only 15% of our brain is grown before birth, and 85% is developed afterwards, so we're far more flexible than we imagine. There are, to be sure, compromises that sabotage our integrity, and others that are prudent and beneficial. Eleanor Roosevelt (1884-1962), American diplomat and activist, used to say: the key in creative compromises is always to compromise *up* not down.

The *Common Ground Network* in Washington, D.C. has offered reconciliation efforts across the divide between pro-life and pro-choice forces. Common Ground constitutes an approach to dialogue in highly conflictual situations. It emphasizes areas of agreement while respecting profound differences. Common Ground is not some mushy, middle ground, but a program that offers opponents a chance to move to "higher ground" by furnishing space "to sit down together, hear each other's stories and re-humanize people on the other side of the chasm." In small groups, participants are invited to share the story of how they came to call themselves pro-choice or pro-life. You see, no one can argue with a person's experience. Frequently, the common denominator is a painful experience, and that's why there exists so much passion and torment around this issue. Common Ground works for people who don't have to produce an enemy in order to do their moral work. Common Ground majors in respectfulness.

Our principal human mission is to be committed neither to the *closed* mind nor to the *empty* mind but to the *open* mind which can shift according to the insights and intuitions of every fresh hour and revelation. One of the first sermons I ever crafted and delivered, back in 1965, was based on the biblical passage where the Aramaic word *ephphatha* (meaning "be opened") was uttered by

Jesus upon healing a person who was both deaf and dumb (Mark 7:34). This exhortation to "be opened" has posed a fruitful mantra throughout the maturation of my spiritual journey. In fact, at the beginning of every worship service, during my years as a settled pastor, I would tender the familiar phrase: "We are a people of open minds, loving hearts, and helping hands." For once we open up our heads, hearts, and hands, it's increasingly difficult to shut or close ourselves back up.

The rabbis of old put it this way: we come into existence with our fists clenched, but when we die, our hands are wide open. The purpose of life is to keep opening up our entire beings, all along the road, from birth toward death.

Ephphatha.

Fifthly, being a truth-seeker isn't sufficient for the full religious life. This has proven to be our Achilles heel as freethinkers. There's nothing wrong with our desire to be truth-seekers as long as we don't halt the search or make a terminal value out of questing. The painter Pablo Picasso, who could hardly be accused of religious dogmatism, saw through the idolatry of searching when it's put in opposition to finding. He wrote: "In my opinion to search means little in painting. To find, is the thing. The one who finds something, no matter what it might be, at least arouses our curiosity, if not our imagination. Therefore, when I paint, my object is to show what I've found and not merely what I'm looking for."

So, as religious reformists, we're seekers *and* finders. Even though our findings are never final, they furnish operating wisdoms to guide our lives. We learn to stake our lives on incomplete knowledge and imperfect vision. Rev. Forrest Church (1948-2009) noted that "almost every important decision I have ever made has been based on 60% convictions. But I do know that not to act, means acting on behalf of that which I don't believe in. I call it the 40% solution."

There's more to this truth business. Having found some truth, Commandment #9 summons us to entertain the consequences of what we've found. Truth-facing is frequently disquieting and at times socially unpopular. As the writer, Mary Flannery O'Connor (1925-1964) quipped: "Find the truth and it shall make you odd!" Yes, there are truths we'd rather ignore: truths about ourselves, our jobs, our inherited beliefs, our families, our friends or lovers, our country, and our value systems. We join together to form congregations precisely because facing and living the truth is so difficult that only with the support of honest and caring companions dare we navigate this arduous commitment.

Proverbs 11:14 in the Hebrew Scriptures puts it candidly: "Where there is no guidance, a people fall; but in an abundance of counselors, there is safety." Not only is safety available, but opportunities for expansion and growth are plentiful. Every last one of us needs "an abundance of counselors" and the steadfast caress and critique of a beloved community.

Once we've found some truth and begun to face some of the truth, then we're impelled to be truth-tellers. Speaking truth to power in a world where truth-telling isn't particularly valued, either privately or publicly, is no stress-free challenge. Most of us can dole out hallmark card sentiments, but the deeper, abrasive truths are hard to tell our mates, buddies, associates, our political or parish leaders, and, of course, ourselves. In the book-banning frenzy in America today, for example, the "anti-woke" fanatics should consider telling the full truth about the Bible, which contains passages of incest, onanism, bestiality, prostitution, genital mutilation, fellatio, rape, and even infanticide.

Recently, I read Nancy Koester's inspiring biography, *We Will Be Free: The Life and Faith of Sojourner Truth* (2023)—undoubtedly, a book that would be forbidden by today's self-righteous zealots. Truth was born into slavery as Isabella Baumfree and was forced into illiteracy. Isabella later fled from her enslavers and took to domestic work. Then, she felt called by the Holy Spirit to become a traveling lecturer and preacher on justice movements such as temperance, abolition, and women's rights.

Isabella Baumfree matured from being a victim to a survivor to a champion. She renamed herself, because Isabella felt God was calling her to convey nothing but the whole and unvarnished truth. And Sojourner Truth boldly did just that, in front of both black and white audiences. When someone questioned Sojourner if she always possessed that name, she declared: "When I left the house of bondage, I left everything behind. I wanted nothing of Egypt on me." Not only was her new name purposeful, it also made it more difficult for slave catchers to track her down. And, furthermore, she mused: "No slave holder can lay any claim to Sojourner Truth, for the truth does not stay where there is any kind of slavery."

She was also a superlative singer of gospel and freedom songs, as well as an ad-libber who used her wit to subdue jeerers and alter minds. Often before her lectures, foes would spread lies such as claiming that she was really a man dressed in a woman's clothes. One man even asked Sojourner Truth to bare her breasts to prove her gender identity. She refused.

Anti-woke peddlers would claim that she "benefitted" from being a slave. No, Sojourner Truth became a servant of God and humanity due to her own tenacity and boundless courage. She benefitted herself and our world by laboring to become a person of unerring truthfulness and abiding compassion ... "an unlettered theologian." Folks would often bemoan that Truth couldn't even read the Scriptures, to which she would cleverly retort: "I have a Bible in me." Sojourner Truth faced every moral controversy head on, because "I go in for agitating." She was the spirited and disquieting forerunner of Ida B. Wells, Mamie Till-Mobley, Fannie Lou Hamer, and Opal Tometi, co-founder of the *Black Lives Matter* movement in 2013.

Twenty-first century pilgrims who aspire to become moral agitators would do well to resemble Sojourner Truth's witness. We need to keep revisiting her life-story to inform and motivate our own behavior as ethical campaigners. When duly heeded, Sojourner Truth's model will awaken our consciences and clean up our households ... starting with my own association of Unitarian Universalism which has been dealing head-on with the truth about our culpability as explicit or unknowing racists, classists, and misogynists.

Telling the truth is more complex and difficult than either telling lies or keeping silent. Nonetheless, at our most honorable, we belong to a faith of heretics who have long-dared to contest the orthodoxies of their day. They've spoken truth to anguish, truth to schmaltz, truth to conflict, and truth to the social, political, and religious party lines and powerholders of their times. May we sign on as tried and true members of this principled tribe.

A New Yorker cartoon reads: "Oh, I could never be a Unitarian; they always try to tell the truth." That may be stretching it a bit, but to be a people of integrity, we cannot live with less than 90%

truth-telling. And when we do dare to speak the truth in love, we're doing so not only for ourselves and neighbors but also in tribute to our religious forebears such as Frances Ellen Watkins Harper, Theodore Parker, Mary Livermore, and Whitney Young, and we're aspiring to set the stage as well as for our descendants.

Finally, we seek after the truth, find and face some, and tell as much as we can. Then we must do the truth. Embodying our truths in our daily life is the litmus test of religion. Note that in Deuteronomy 16:20, justice is doubly reinforced as the summary imperative: "Justice, and only justice, you shall follow, that you may live and inherit the land which the Lord your God gives you." Christian scriptures exhort us, above all else, "to do the truth," not just chat about it, pay homage to it, or fuss with it. We're ultimately summoned to be *truthers*. Or as one of my teenage compatriots put it: "I'm just trying to follow my feet!"

I hesitate to criticize one of the premier sages of human history, Buddha, but I would amend one of his statements: "The mind is everything. What you think you become." First off, the brain, by itself, isn't everything; our mind hankers for the creative and constructive companionship of the body, the heart, the spirit, the conscience, and the soul. We function optimally as a unified being, a whole Self.

Second, there are oodles of self-care experts who would second Buddha's contention by proffering similar claims such as "change your life by changing your thoughts" or "you become what you think." Such claims are half-baked truths. Much of our life does indeed launch in the mind, and rightly so. However, without enactment, our ideas can devolve into empty-headed whims.

The key to a virtuous existence rests in our courage to personify noble thoughts in our daily behavior. We are bidden to focus upon behavior over dogma, orthopraxy rather than orthodoxy. Our true character is revealed in our conduct not in our excitements or decrees. And, in the African-American tradition, worship is never over until parishioners obtain their marching orders, wherein they're implored to go forth and "tangibilitate" the day's lessons!

"Facebook" connections are important, but they pale next to greeting another person face-to-face. Our world is loaded with bystanders, those who loll about ... living just this side of engagement. They say that children remember 20% of what they hear, 30% of what they see, 50% of what they see and hear, 70% of what say, and 90% of what they do. This isn't startling data, because the figures run pretty much the same for adults. A creative, compassionate, courageous world demands more of its inhabitants than being Face-bookers or onlookers. If and when a judgment day arrives, the focus won't be on our brilliant or noble thoughts, or even the range of our mystical epiphanies, but upon our bold and gutsy acts of joy-sharing, peace-making, and justice-building. Embodiment will be the acid test of our earthly sojourn.

Note some praiseworthy *truthers* in American history. In the suffragist and abolitionist era, women such as Clara Barton, Harriet Tubman, and Elizabeth Cady Stanton were enterprising truth-doers, well into their senior years. In large measure, these ardent feminists (many of whom were practicing Unitarians or Universalists) lived energetic and lengthy lives because they were occupied with sizable spiritual challenges. They stayed morally employed. They kept asking: "What will best serve the universe today?" rather than fixating upon their own personal needs. They dismantled their "vertical coffins" and realized meaningful deeds.

Women weren't "given" the vote; they had to march forth and "grab" it. Our fore-sisters knew that progress was not inevitable. They had to make it happen. Yet in 2025, disenfranchisement is alive and well. Voter suppression remains a perilous hurdle, especially for Black, Indigenous, and People of Color (BIPOC), in our alleged "land of the free and home of the brave."

American social reformer Susan B. Anthony (1820-1906) once said that she wished "to live another century and see the fruition of all the work for women's rights." Although she never got the right to vote herself, I've always been inspired by the manner in which she completed her life-journey. During the last 48 hours of her existence, Anthony faintly voiced the names of suffragists who labored alongside her, knowns and unknowns, in a veritable roll call. Susan B. was acknowledging each and every one of her co-conspirators. There's no finer way to finish life than with heartfelt, spoken appreciation.

And we would be remiss, if we didn't pay homage to Universalist Judith Sargent Murray, feminist essayist, poet, and commentator of considerable note who died in 1820, the same year that Anthony was born. In her essay entitled "On the Equality of the Sexes," Murray wrote: "Yes ... our souls are by nature equal to yours; the same breath of God animates, enlivens, and invigorates us ..." Judith was ambitious on her own while remaining spirited on behalf of her husband, John. Among the admiring subscribers were John Adams, George and Martha Washington, and Benjamin Franklin.

Here's the valiant witness of another feminist honoree. In 1861, Olympia Brown arrived at St. Lawrence Theological School to study for the ministry, startling the seminary President who thought he had discouraged her from enrolling. After becoming the first woman to be denominationally ordained (as a Universalist) in 1863, Brown became an advocate for the right of women to vote. It was not until 1920, at the age of 85, that Rev. Olympia was able to cast her first ballot.

Lest I leave our brothers out, let's turn to a telling example from the Unitarian heritage. William Ellery Channing (1780-1842) practiced spiritual disciplines throughout his life, yet his personal piety was maintained for one reason alone: to effect cultural change. He directed the substance of his ministerial career not only to informing minds and transforming souls but also to reforming the structures of society. Channing's causes ranged from child labor to alcoholism, slavery to juvenile delinquency. He was also deeply concerned for both prisoners and the poor. William Ellery agreed with Ralph Waldo Emerson that "ideas are tangible things to be lived." So he lived freedom, lived justice, and lived mercy, however imperfectly.

What's exemplary about Channing was his willingness to progress as a prophetic presence. So, he kept on evolving morally and spiritually all the way to his crypt. Perhaps his foremost growth as a minister occurred with respect to his anti-slavery work. Channing was profoundly impressed with Lydia Maria Child's viewpoints on slavery espoused in the first anti-slavery book published in America: *An Appeal in Favor of that Class of Americans Called Africans* (1833).

Channing was so captivated by Child's book, that, despite ill health, he walked a couple miles to her place to discuss the issue. After a three-hour conversation, William Ellery credited Child with goading his conscience to speak out on the question, even if not as zealously as Child desired. Lydia regularly chastised her religious sympathizers with stinging words:

> *I find Unitarianism a mere half-way house, where spiritual travelers find themselves well accommodated for the night, but where they grow weary of spending the day.*

Never a full-bore abolitionist, Channing pushed to bring an end to slavery in his "calm, self-controlled, benevolent" way. In the final analysis, Channing's views on slavery proved too drastic for the alienated Unitarian conservatives and too tepid for the radical abolitionists. Channing preached, week after week, to stodgy, stubborn Bostonians nudging the most recalcitrant toward "cheerful, vigorous, beneficent action of each for all." He was a moderate with courage, what progressive theologian Jack Mendelsohn called "a civilized controversialist." Channing embodied truth, however tentatively and timidly.

Evolutionary justice has been echoed as well in the Universalist heritage. Benjamin Rush (1746-1813), signer of the Declaration of Independence, physician, social reformer, and fervent supporter of the Enlightenment, always talked about our country's destiny in progressive terms: "A belief has arisen that the American Revolution is over. This is so far from being the case that we have only finished the first act of the great drama." In 2025, America confronts multiple "revolutions" of moral gravity, so it's sobering to recall the sentiments of Rush affirming that society *and* religion are inherently developmental processes. Both remain incomplete, vulnerable, and ever-evolving.

We're required not to think or visualize revolutionary justice but to perform justice every waking moment of our life, not merely when we feel like it. Minor or major deeds suffice. Private and public actions qualify. Our conduct will always reveal our dogmas. The Psalmist exclaims: "Compassion is where peace and justice kiss."

When I think of justice, my heart revisits 1965 Selma: the spirit, the solidarity, and the sacrifices. This historic March expanded my mind, fortified my heart, emboldened my soul, and rocked my conscience forever. I concur with the contention of fellow marcher, S. Hunter Leggitt, in addressing the younger generation: "If I could give each of you just one gift for a lifetime, it would be to have spent that week in Selma!"

In 1965, when Martin Luther King, Jr.'s clarion call rang forth "to put your body where the trouble is," especially targeting sympathetic, white Americans, my hand cautiously rose, and I boarded the bus for the cross-country trek from San Francisco to Selma, my first ever foray into the South.

I was a bookish and pious, 23-year-old, seminary greenhorn, unformed in the rigors of justice-building, let alone "a communist-trained anarchist," to use Governor George Wallace's damning phrase. In retrospect, I went because of two spiritual sparks: WWJD ("What would Jesus do?") reinforced by WWMS ("What would Mother say?"). My decision seemed in alignment with both the Nazarene and my moral activist Mom, who later remarked: "Tommy, I've never been prouder of you than when you showed up in Selma!"

Upon arrival, *Southern Christian Leadership Conference* rules steered our ground mission: (1) Commit to non-violence practice; and (2) Do whatever needs to be done. If you can't obey these two directives, we kindly invite you to get back on your bus and return home. Accordingly, we seminarians weren't "foot-soldiers" (except for the final leg into Montgomery) but rather "field-laborers" (clearing pastures of cow-dung while daily setting up tents for the marchers). Our bodies grew bone weary even as our souls were set ablaze.

We remember Selma whenever we honor unknown slaves and unsung resisters throughout American history. We remember Selma whenever we admit we're part of the problem as we sit in seats of privilege in predominantly white institutions and that we can be part of the solution whenever we redistribute power and resources from those very same seats. We remember Selma whenever we combat existing forms of economic, social, racial, political, and environmental oppression. We remember Selma whenever we're color-sensitive rather than naively claiming to be color-blind.

The civil rights campaigners whom I met in Selma in 1965 were willing to risk their jobs, their homes, and even their lives in the unyielding pursuit of creating and sustaining the Beloved Community—an evolving reality that aspires to welcome, yea embrace, all colors and capacities, orientations and convictions. As John Lewis, one of King's stoutest colleagues, put it:

Consider those two words. "Beloved"—not hateful, not violent, not uncaring, not unkind. And "Community"—not separate, not polarized, not adversarial.

Fifty years later, I returned to Selma, with my life-mate, Carolyn, to commemorate our homeland's protracted struggle for racial justice, joining 70,000 demonstrators (including President Barack Obama) on Bloody Sunday, as we marched across the Edmund Pettis Bridge.

The first week in 1965 launched my irreversible, albeit inconsistent, journey toward wholeness. This second week in 2015 sent me home with fortified resolve to keep on marching all the way to my grave. I renewed my vows as a civil rights' veteran fighting for "liberty and justice for all." *Semper fidelis* ("always faithful") as the Marines put it. Trudging resolutely and fiercely onward ... I remain a flawed lifer for human equality. Now in 2025, as I envision new marching orders, I'm not sure where I'll be dispatched and in what local fields I might serve. I'm simply trying to stay awake and accountable as an ally and accomplice, willing to put my aging body wherever the trouble might be.

Both personally and societally, we white activists still reside but one gesture, one lapse, one word, and one moment of falsehood or lethargy away from intensifying racism in America. We must remain on duty as moral sentinels to sustain the courageous struggle of Selma, "keeping our eyes on the prize" and "holding on" as the spiritual beckons. We're summoned to remember that the nonviolence of Dr. Martin Luther King, Jr. was neither passive nor weak-kneed, but tough-minded and tender-hearted.

Fifty-seven years after King's murder, it's tempting to forget or ignore his demands for a fundamental restructuring of American society. King's embodiment of truth was not sentimental but revolutionary. He kept warning fellow Americans about the triple evils of "racism, militarism, and materialism." King took a radical stand on Vietnam when advised by both his black and white cohorts to be silent and stick to race relations. Instead Martin replied: "It's worthless to talk about integration, if there's no world to integrate. The bombs in Vietnam explode at home. They destroy the hopes and possibilities for a decent America."

Without a doubt, it's awkward to immortalize any reformer, and

King was flawed to be sure: wrestling with despair, smoking and drinking constantly, and womanizing as ways to garner relief from living under the constant threat of death and vicious attacks on his character by black and non-black writers and politicians alike. At this precarious juncture in American history, we desperately need campaigners who intrepidly tread the moral path. As professor of religion and social transformation, Vincent Harding (1931-2014), keenly noted: "King was a morally inconvenient hero." Might you and I pledge daily to be "morally inconvenient" in some way?

I've closed my reflections on commandment #9, focusing on Dr. King, because, despite the severe inner and outer agony of his life, King found comfort in the conviction that the struggle itself was right. In his effort "to do the will of God," King could lose himself and prepare, prematurely, to lay down his life. He said: "the quality, not the longevity, of one's life is what's important. If you're cut down in a movement that's designed to save the soul of a nation, then no other death could be more redemptive."

King was nonviolent to the end. Indeed, at the close of his life, he was murdered in Memphis, Tennessee, while peacefully protesting with sanitation workers in support of their just cause. Martin Luther King, Jr. pursued truth, spoke truth, and lived truth to the fullest extent of his 39 years on earth.

Study questions for personal reflection and/or group discussion

(1) Describe moments when you feel obliged to withhold the full truth?

(2) Are there lies or half-truths that have bedeviled your life? Share.

(3) Address the Adrienne Rich (1929-2012) quote: "Lying is done with words and also with silence."

(4) Ponder the relevance of each phrase of the statement: "Is it true, is it necessary, and is it kind?"

(5) What are the primary modes (e.g. science, reason, revelation, intuition, and action) through which you have pursued and realized truth?

(6) Comment upon the distinctions between an empty, closed, and open mind?

(7) Describe a few situations when you have changed your mind? And why?

(8) How have you practiced the art of constructive compromise over the years?

(9) Amplify upon the imperatives of truthfulness—seeking, finding, facing, telling, and doing truth—in your own daily life.

(10) Describe some of the lessons of Sojourner Truth and Martin Luther King, Jr. for the conduct of your current life?

Chapter X

Cling to Naught

X. Thou shall not covet your neighbor's house; your
neighbor's wife, or manservant, or maidservant,
or ox, or ass, or anything that is your neighbor's ...
—Exodus 20:17

Saints and birds don't collect.
—Neem Karoli Baba (1900-1973)

*Be content with what you have:
rejoice in the way things are.
When you realize there is nothing lacking,
the whole world belongs to you.*
—Lao Tzu

We've arrived at the final commandment which focuses more on attitude than action. In a strange yet compelling way, it reinforces the thrust of the first one as well. Commandment #1 charges us not to worship other *gods*, and commandment #10 exhorts us not to covet the *goods* of others. Every conceivable *good* in our neighbor's house is recorded here—except plants, silverware, any pets, and the dining room table. Actually, "anything" is specified! When we become either idle worshippers or greedy possessors, we're thrown back into slavery. Our possessions, or those of another, begin to possess us. As with the Israelites, we've been set free to rejoice and serve, serve and rejoice. Covetousness spells bondage.

A neighbor once spotted Abraham Lincoln trying to separate two of his sons, locked in a bloody-nosed battle. "What's the matter, Mr. Lincoln?" "Just what's the matter with the whole world," Abe answered. "I've got three walnuts, and each boy wants two." We all covet something of somebody's at some time. We're avaricious beings. The Buddha warned: insatiability is comparable to salty water; the more we guzzle, the thirstier we become. Even if we imbibe the entire ocean, we will remain thirsty. Greed is a self-defeating endeavor.

"The prosperity Gospel" of televangelists is an example of covetousness run amok. Cathleen Falsani, religion columnist for the *Chicago Sun-Times*, rightly calls it to account:

> In the Gospel of Saint Matthew, we are told that Jesus said, "You cannot serve both God and money." The "prosperity gospel," an insipid heresy, teaches that God blesses those God favors most with material wealth.

Well, no God worthy of the name operates that way. Yahweh is hardly some financial advisor who enriches the fortune of favorites. Remember the Israelites were regularly seduced into worshipping the golden calf. The same temptation lures modern day spiritual devotees.

I know of no better antidote to the pernicious demon of covetousness than genuine contentment. Our mission is to make sufficient peace with our own situation so that we might be free to admire without turning avaricious and to respect without coveting the possessions or the personhood of our neighbors. In sum, the key to a joyful journey is to want what we have and be who we are.

Here's a Yiddish folktale about the family in Budapest who went to their rabbi with a complaint: "Life is unbearable. There are nine of us living in one room. What can I do?" The rabbi answers: "Well, take your goat into the room with you." The family is incredulous, but the rabbi insists: "Do as I say and come back in a week." A week later the family comes back, looking more agitated than before. "We can't stand it," they tell the rabbi. "The goat is filthy." The rabbi then tells them, "Go home and let the goat out and come back in a week."

A radiant clan returns to the rabbi a week later, exclaiming: "Life is beautiful. We enjoy every minute of it now that there's no goat, only the nine of us!" Yes, equanimity would exhort us to accept life as it is and to make sufficient peace with our current conditions. We would be wise to quit fighting reality.

Before we explore two primary elements of the healthy and holy existence—generosity and contentedness—let's address the yoked demons of jealousy and envy, direct relatives of covetousness. Jealousy constitutes the fear of losing something or not wanting to share something or someone you possess or hope to possess. As Margaret Wheatley (1944-) American writer, speaker, and organizational consultant states:

> *If jealousy dominates, we turn inward, shrivel our hearts and lose strength. If generosity grows, our world expands. We realize there's enough to go around. Jealousy is such a waste of a good human heart.*

Envy, the green-eyed monster is a festering, resentful longing for another's advantages or achievements. It produces a debilitating case of the "if-onlies": if only I possessed this or if only I could do that. And plenty of folks (including myself) are bedeviled by the related phenomenon called FOMO ("fear of missing out").

Envy is poisonous, because we aspire to be someone else and have what they have or be who they are ... when our life-purpose is to "be true to thy self!" We're placed on earth to count our own blessings not those of another. Envy destroys our capacity to be grateful, because we never have enough. We become, as we say in English, "eaten up by envy." Devoured.

Envy and jealousy are sometimes used interchangeably in modern Bible translations, although they differ slightly. Envy is a reaction to lacking something that another person has. Jealousy is a reaction to the fear or threat of losing something or someone, we currently enjoy.

Envy is the sixth deadly sin, because it destroys our sense of personal peace, without which, no greater harmony can be achieved. As Proverbs 14:30 relates:

> *A sound heart is life to the body, but envy is rottenness to the bones.*

Although there is such a matter as "godly jealousy" (II Corinthians 11:2), the scriptures never review envy positively. I beg to differ. In Buddhist culture, "appreciative joy" is the corrective to envy. There's a compelling case for benign envy which can become a motivating force in our moral evolution. Admiration is normal and healthy. Certain examples and deeds that our neighbors display are worth envying, then emulating.

We're not self-sufficient creatures; we become inspired by the beauty and behavior of others. Envy can be utilized for good whenever we respect the insights of scholars or the efforts of social servants ... arousing us to pursue "the better angels of our nature." In non-material covetousness, envy can be a growth-inducing power. We just need to apply our envy to a higher rather than a lower cause.

And religions can profoundly benefit from inter-faith discourse. Rev. Dr. Barbara Brown Taylor makes a compelling case in her book, *Holy Envy*, for every spiritual pilgrim gleaning insights from other traditions rather than falling prey to self-sufficiency.

> *... holy envy alerts me to things in other religions that have become neglected in my own, thoughts that may go by different names.*

This judicious perspective harkens back to the first commandments where we're bidden to recognize that no one owns God. Since no religious tradition captures the fullness of God; we can, and must, gain wisdom from one another. It's tempting to grow conceited with our chosen "lurking-places" of the one God. The words of the Infinite One in Isaiah 55:8-9 rouse us out of such arrogance:

> *For my thoughts are not your thoughts, nor are your ways my ways. For as the heavens are higher than the earth, so are my ways higher than your ways and my thoughts than your thoughts.*

Sobering and humbling news.

In short, we progressives draw inspiration from world-wide heritages. Our values are grounded in manifold sources: East and West, North and South, ancient and modern, secular and spiritual. Our major 21st century task is to contribute towards the creation of a globe of greater multi-religious dialogue and harmony.

Our planet urgently needs humans who transcend tribalism and migrate toward *universalism*. We can only accomplish this mission by spending time with siblings of other faith traditions and cultures, mental and social capacities, races and gender identities, engaging in compassionate conversation and collaborative action.

Now, let's welcome two supreme spiritual practices that diminish covetousness. First, generosity; then, contentedness.

As Rev. Gary Smith, succinctly claims:

> *Generosity equals large living and stinginess equals small living.*

Humans tend to collect resentments. We overdose on our own opinions. We even stockpile friends. The only corrective to such greed is generosity which reduces our fruitless tendencies to covet and cling. Big-heartedness enables us to rise above parsimony. When our heart softens and opens up, so do our heads and hands. We become less ego-driven and far freer.

Cornel West (1953-), American philosopher and political activist, phrases it this way:

> *Everybody here has already been paid for. All you have to do is prepare yourself so that you can pay for someone else who is yet to come and act on it, act with kindness and courtesy and generosity.*

Truly, the key to meeting the imperatives of all Ten Commandments banks upon our capacity to share our personal wealth, far and wide. I worded it this way in a recent *Tanka* (Japanese) poem, a 5 line (5/7/5/7/7) syllable count form, for my *Conscious Aging* seminar:

Magnanimity
Opening the heart
Graying, greening gracefully
Blooming bountifully
Bestowing gifts lavishly
As magnanimous ocean

Archibald MacLeish's play *J.B.* unequivocally declares: "We got the earth for nothing." Therefore, the gracious and generous response is to give back to the blessed creation everything we have and are, all the way home, and count not the cost. Our generosity begins with enjoying ourselves, then spreading the overflow. Generosity isn't an attempt to repay the creation in full; that's impossible. We're bountiful, because our cup is full and yearns to spill and spill and spill and spill ...

The longer I walk this earth, the more I realize that generosity underwrites all the other virtues. As the Buddhists crisply put it: "Generosity first." Why? Because without generosity, one loves sparingly; without generosity, one acts for justice rarely; and without generosity, one grows miserly of treasure, time, and talent—the cardinal gifts of our heart. I fall short as a person, partner, parent, professional, and pilgrim—yet every day I keep on churning, since my life will ultimately be measured by the size of my munificence. On my epitaph I desire the passage of the English gravestone:

"What I gave, I have. What I spent, I had. What I kept, I lost." Truly, we are the sum of our gifts.

Did you know that the words genius and generous come from the Latin root "*genere*" meaning "to beget?" Therefore, any genius for life denotes the ability to generate warmth and well-being in others. Generative people are generous of heart, charitable of spirit, and abundant in soulfulness. Generous people are likely to experience the gratification of seeing some wrongs battled, prejudices countered, sorrows lightened, and institutions upheld ... while they're still buzzing.

We can bloom and bestow in multiple ways, both materially and spiritually. As the illustrious Roman philosopher, Epictetus (circa 55-135 CE), taught: "Never suppress a generous impulse!" I have no quarrel with the philosopher. The drive to become progressively unselfish is my homeward quest.

Many Native cultures measure prosperity not by what we possess but by what we're able to hand on. They celebrate *potlach*, or the great giveaway, where objects are liberally distributed to the neediest in the larger community. We're doing that as well, in our own household, shedding and sharing with family and friends as well as giving items weekly to the homeless center where I volunteer. This mode of *potlach* is particularly meaningful when I view clients walking off with our donated apparel or canned goods.

Ultimately, there will be our last *potlach*: the giving away of our entire corpus back to the earth from whence we came. Other animals do it. Buffaloes bestow all their parts—flesh, hide, and horns—for the benefit of kindred. Trees compost the soil. An ever-evolving love summons all of us two-leggeds to sow, plant, and harvest, then give away the bounty of our being upon death.

Here's another way to reflect upon "spilling out our treasure," based on a piece from May Sarton (1912-1995), prolific Belgian-American poet:

> *I would like to believe when I die that I have given myself away like a tree that sows seeds every spring and never counts the loss, because it is not a loss, it is adding to future life ... strongly rooted perhaps, but spilling out its treasure on the wind.*

I confess to relishing the hope that my death might "add to future life." That's my plan and wish, spilling out whatever treasures I might either own or embody back to the earth as well as into the hearts of future generations. Going forth ... giving generously!

Second, we turn to living with a temperament of essential contentedness. Fulfillment is never found in another's car or dog, achievements or stature. May we dwell in the world, exploring and admiring its bounteous gifts, without needing to own every parcel. At some point, we need to say: "I have and am enough!" The Buddhists call this state: dissolving into the eventual stillness or "clinging to naught."

I'm reminded of the Hebrew concept of *dayenu* which means "it would have been sufficient or enough." It's integral to the Jewish Seder ritual and part of the song that if God had only delivered us from Egypt, it would have been enough. If God had only given us the Torah, the five books of Moses, it would have been enough. If God had only given us the Sabbath, it would have been enough.

What is enough for each of us? What are our critical needs: food, shelter, vocation, justice, and love? What else would we desire as a staple in our diet? The truth is that not everyone has access to life's necessities—the raw material, the tools, and the disciplines to conduct a satisfying life, so it's our human mission to insure that what belongs to people gets to them.

I recall in my ministry a touching exchange between a father and daughter in their last moments together at our San Diego airport; the girl is going away to college and her father is dying. Standing near the security gate, they hugged and the father said, "I love you, Gretchen, and I wish you enough." The daughter replied, "Dad, our life together has been more than enough. Your love is all I ever needed. On your next voyage, I wish you enough too, Dad!"

Dayenu.

There is a clear-cut distinction between covetousness and contentedness. To be content means to avoid obsessions yet still pursue our deep, driving desires. As the Hindu *Upanishads* fruitfully state:

> *You are what your deepest desire is.*
> *As your desire is, so is your intention.*
> *As your intention is, so is your will.*
> *As your will is so is your deed.*

To prioritize my worthy desires, I've chosen, as an elder, to pay homage to Rabbi Zalman Schacter-Shalomi's (1924-2021) classic *Bill of Fare*:

(1) *What do you wish to taste again?*
(2) *What do you wish to enjoy for the first time?*
(3) *What do you choose to stomach no longer?*
(4) *What would be a healthy spiritual diet for the rest of your life?*

What might be the elements of your *Bill of Fare* at this stage in your life-journey?

My mother was a poster person for serenity, remaining essentially content throughout the entirety of her almost 96 years on this planet. Mom wasn't always untroubled and cloudless, since she bit her nails, just as I pick my nose. Perhaps you have an irksome habit as well. Nonetheless, Mother Mary routinely exemplified the virtue that the Shona tribe in Zimbabwe calls *rufaro*: an unshakable sense of equanimity. Neither highs nor lows appeared to jangle mom's cage. The Hebrew equivalent translates as "calmness of the soul." My mother possessed it.

Mom wasn't a fatalist, because she passionately labored for constructive changes in her world. She wasn't passive or acquiescent. Resonating with Dr. Martin Luther King, Jr.'s phrase "creative maladjustment" kept our mother ethically responsive and spiritually sane. She was a relentless campaigner for racial equality, and the only person on her Presbyterian Church session who stood tall for gay liberation and rights from the 1970s forward. Mom was a quiet yet persevering radical. She would have received one of the "shameless agitator" awards that our congregation in San Diego has handed out annually.

Most of the time, Mom gave up wanting what she didn't already have and learned how to bear what she couldn't alter. She accepted the workings of the universe; then, she aligned herself with them. Mary Catherine Flanagan Towle straddled being content but never satisfied. In the nursing home at the end of her bed was a small table upon which stood a photo of her beloved husband, Harold, of 54 years, and snapshots of my brother and me, alongside a Bible opened up to Philippians 4:11:

I have learned to be contented in whatever circumstances I am.

Mom's sense of repose was shown in her willingness to die when her time came. She was neither fascinated by nor fixated on her death; she rarely referenced it. Yet as death drew nigh, Mother Mary faced it not with rage, resentment, or regret, but with abundant *rufaro*.

When former United States president Jimmy Carter turned 90, he confirmed that his soul could rest in peace if two of his aspirations were accomplished before he died. First, there would be peace in the Middle East, and second, the Guinea worm disease would be eliminated. Since 1986, The Carter Center has led a vigorous international campaign, in collaboration with other world-wide organizations, to rid the globe of this devastating infection. Alas, when Jimmy died in 2024, at the age of 100, the first objective of Middle East peace remained unrealized, but the Guinea worm illness drew extremely close to becoming only the second disease in history, after small pox, to be eradicated.

Moral persistence, resulting in contentedness, is stunningly illustrated in the odyssey of Jimmy Carter. Would that more of us elders and crones were tenacious enough to follow in the path of Carter's gospel: "My faith demands that I do whatever I can, whenever I can, for as long as I can, with whatever I have to give, to make a difference in the world."

As I meander down the homestretch and embrace my own mortality, my lodestar has become the *Serenity Prayer* composed in 1943 by liberal theologian, Reinhold Niebuhr, for a church service in a New England town where he was serving as the pastor. Years later, in 1948, this supplication became the mantra of the *Alcoholics Anonymous* recovery movement. Hallmark Cards utilized it in its 1962 *Graduation Line*, reimbursing Niebuhr for the rights. And, fatefully, it even became the official slogan of the West German Army Academy after World War II. But we dare not overlook its original context and mission.

The Serenity Prayer was composed at the height of World War II, when Niebuhr became an early and forthright critic of Nazism. In her superlative memoir, *The Serenity Prayer: Faith and Politics in Times of Peace and War (2003)*, Niebuhr's own daughter, author, and publisher, Elizabeth Sifton (1939-2019), identifies the prayer as more than a self-focused refrain. It was an appeal for "collective action for collective betterment":

> *The Serenity Prayer was composed in wartime, and it*
> *also addresses the inconsolable pain, loss, and guilt*
> *that war inflicts on the communities that wage it;*
> *it goes to the heart of the possibilities and impossibilities*
> *of collective action for collective betterment—that is to say,*
> *to the heart of the possibilities for peace.*

Yes, pursuing greater internal, interpersonal, and international peace was the supreme goal of Niebuhr's entreaty.

In his career as both parish minister and seminary professor, Niebuhr spoke out and acted against all forms of bigotry and injustice. Consequently, this prayer was crafted as an imperative for repairing both our inner spirit *and* our outer conduct. Can you imagine a more pertinent prayer as we unpack the moral challenges posed by the Ten Commandments for our own personal and public lives in the 21st century?

Furthermore, the Serenity Prayer carries immense relevance for our closing laps on earth, precisely when we're summoned to welcome contentedness. Dwelling in a sufficiently serene, accepting, courageous, and wise state is essential to one's consummation ... whether we're healing relational harm, serving a social cause, altering our life-choices, sorting out family finances and heirlooms, crooning a ballad, or garnering an untroubled night's sleep.

My daily aim remains to ensoul the message of this foundational prayer (Niebuhr's version):

God, give us the serenity to accept what cannot be changed;
Give us the courage to change what should be changed;
Give us the wisdom to distinguish one from the other.

So, here I am, a full-blown elder, rounding third base and dashing (make that, clambering) straightway toward home plate. But I'm no longer preoccupied with scoring the winning run and soaking in the cheers of the roaring crowd. Simply reaching home base—the place of my origin, "everlasting love"—will suffice.

A primary quality of a "good death: is going gently. Hence, I quibble with Dylan Thomas (1914-1953), Welsh poet, whose most famous piece was:

Do not go gentle into that good night,
old age should burn and rave at close of day;
rage, rage against the dying of the light.

During my homestretch years, there may well come a time to "burn and rave" as bodily windows squeak and doors shut. Nonetheless, my desire remains to close out life quietly—traveling ever-so gently into the next stage. Dying skyward or dying earthward, entering the light or entering the darkness—either route will suit me just fine. My sole aspiration is peacefully returning to the loving Source of All.

For me, an equivalence of gentleness is softness. The Zen master Dogen, in 1227, traveling back to Japan after spending many years in China with great Zen masters, was asked what he had learned about the process of living-and-dying. And he calmly offered: "Softness of heart, softness of heart."

Miles Beauchamp, a journalist member of one of my interim congregations, frames it movingly:

Water is soft, fluid, and extremely strong.
It will carve away rock. It is strong, patient, and never ceasing.
Be soft, flowing, and surrounding life.

On the road back-home toward death, may our hearts be gentle and soft without being sappy. A sound farewell mantra, called DROPS, beckons: "Don't Resist Or Push, Soften!" Be like water.

As our brain, heart, and limbs irreversibly age, may a sense of contentedness pervade our souls. May we dwell in a state of what the Buddhists fittingly call "calm abiding." May we garner sufficient peace—free, at last, from futile churning or rampant fears, and may we harmonize with what is, with what is, with what is ...

Truly, you and I are helpless both at moment of birth and at moment of death. Our final earthly assignment is to surrender to the earth and to God, the mysteries that fashioned us. The word surrender is derived from "render" which means to give back. Our very existence is a pure and precious gift. We don't own our "being": we've been blessed to possess it for a stretch. Our dying act is tenderly returning our body to its Source.

I pay close heed to the prophet Mohammed's (571-632 A.D.) four crucial words: "True religion is surrender." Pretty much everything has been felt, thought, preached, and done in the name of religion—rapture, brutality, compassion, and subservience. Yet, religion, at its truest, means shedding physicality, releasing outcomes, canning biases, abandoning dreams, even posthumous hopes and submitting our all ... back, back, back to an ever-expanding, benevolent Cosmos. Surrendering, ah surrendering ... easing more graciously into contentment.

As a senior in the midst of taking a slew of final exams, I confess to being a high-control guy. Trust isn't normally my optimal condition. Yet, I'm shifting glacially, surrendering pieces and moments of control and coveting. I'm acknowledging that impermanence is the human condition, and ownership is a fantasy. I'm lightening my load and "hallowing my diminishments" as Pierre Teilhard de Chardin (1881-1955), French philosopher and Jesuit priest, deftly expresses. Gradually, I'm letting *go* (acknowledging the hurts and hallelujahs, hassles and hopes of my past); letting *be* (taking up residence in the eternal now); and letting *come* (welcoming unknown tomorrows). I'm reasonably contented. I'm steadily flowing into eternal peace.

Life is finally about pledging our trust while wandering the earth— experiencing the delights and addressing the core commandments of existence. For a sense of unshakable trust in the Creation and in one another surely makes love achievable and death endurable.

Study questions for personal reflection and/or group discussion

(1) How have you shown yourself to be a *covetous* person?
(2) Are there ways in which *envy* has inspired you to pursue and obtain higher goals?
(3) Scrutinize, phase by phase, the quotation by former United States president Jimmy Carter and its relevance for your life?
(4) How has your journey been a generous and magnanimous one? Brag some.
(5) In what ways have you been stingy or parsimonious? Be honest.
(6) Are you shedding stuff (both physical and spiritual belongings) in your present life? What and how?
(7) What are the deep desires of your current *Bill of Fare*?
(8) In what ways have you grown contented with who you are and what you possess at this stage in your life?
(9) Are you preparing any form of *potlach*? Tell us about it.
(10) Address any relevance of the *Serenity Prayer* for your life.
(11) In what ways are you consciously embracing, as well as preparing, for your own death?

Epilogue

*Do not be daunted by the enormity of the world's grief.
Do justly, now. Love mercy, now. Walk humbly, now.
You are not obliged to complete the work, but neither
are you free to abandon it.*
—Adapted from the Mishnah, Pirkei Avot 2:15-16

*Have so big a mission that it is impossible, and you will fail
and, hence, learn new ways of courage and persistence.*
—Rev. Sean Dennison

My first book, *Generation to Generation: Passing along the Good Life to Your Children* (1986) was comprised of 52 love-letters to our four offspring and based on what Jewish culture calls "an ethical will." Fittingly, *Living with Purpose and Integrity: A Fresh Perspective on the Ten Commandments* (2025) delivers my last will and testament, aspiring to illuminate the Decalogue for contemporary eyes and ears as well as for future generations.

Re-examining and re-energizing these ten imperatives sculpted and delivered approximately 3500 years ago, has been a woolly yet galvanizing valediction. My goal has been to engage this ancient moral code with a moist mind and a cavernous heart. Employing the Ten Commandments, I've aspired to grapple with the nuances and ambiguities of living a more authentic version of myself during my homestretch. After all, I'm an incurable crusader, what's called an *ameliorist*, a reformer who, despite flaws and foibles, believes that the world can be improved (not perfected) by human efforts.

One of my dearest buddies, Charlie O'Leary, was a superb clinical psychologist and, often when my ministerial mind or spirit was flagging, I would enter his counsel chamber. And Dr. Charlie would prod me:

> *Tom, everything you do matters; sometimes it works, sometimes it doesn't, but it always matters. So keep showing self-restraint, kindness, and patience.*
>
> *Everything you do matters!*

Thank you, beloved brother of blessed memory, for planting me on course.

Wisdom submits that the redemption of any culture launches with the redemption of every constituent. Now, I won't be so bold-faced as to assert that, in this modest book, I've redeemed myself, let alone our country or globe, but, hopefully, it might furnish a commendable start for refining our contemporary character and conduct. If salvation seems a tad pretentious, then, at least, may we prove to be gutsy commandment-wrestlers, and, when predictably falling short of fulfillment, seek some forgiveness or what Horace Bushnell (1802-1876), prominent American Protestant minister and theologian, called "our deepest need and highest achievement."

My favorite passage in Christian scriptures is I Corinthians 13, verses 7 and 8 which read as follows:

Love always protects, always trusts,
always hopes, always perseveres.
Love never fails.
(New International Version, 2011)

Well, while love, in its idealized embodiment, may "always" protect, trust, hope, and persevere, as well as never fail, our earthly versions fall short. You and I consistently falter in our loving and being loved; so we need to experience forgiveness, "the final form of love." (Reinhold Niebuhr)

Forgiveness is life's invitation to redress failure through an arduous process that cannot be sidestepped or shortchanged. Forgiveness sets us free. Forgiveness allows our sacred quest to begin again and again and again, voyaging from rupture toward repair. The Jewish view of forgiveness is contained in a verb that pervades its penitential literature, namely, the word: *shuv*, meaning "to turn or to return."

In the staggering sweep of our lives, we continually wipe off our tears and dirt, rise from the ground, and deign to negotiate a "turned-around" life. We seek to keep on failing forward ... beginning again. The biblical doctrine of forgiveness is hopeful, forecasting our ability to turn from evil to good and from alienation toward reconciliation, step by step by step by step, or as my wise brother phrases it—peace-by-peace-by-peace—until we die ... and who knows what might happen then?

Without the blessing of forgiveness, we're never fully released from the consequences of what we've done or what's been done to us. We remain enslaved. Forgiveness *and* freedom are yoked virtues. And note that the Hebrew word for Eygpt, *Mitzrayim,* means "the narrow places" and refers to all the restrictive states—physical, emotional, and spiritual—in which we acknowledge ourselves to be trapped or imprisoned.

This holy Decalogue was crafted precisely for a people recently freed from bondage (400 years' worth!) in Egypt. Consequently, this ageless canon stands ready to help us moderns remove impediments on the path toward greater self-actualization. Rabbi Nachman of Breslov (1772-1810) zeroed in on the human condition with these words:

> *The Exodus from Egypt occurs in every human being,*
> *in every era, in every year, and in every day.*

The Ten Commandments, when resourcefully interpreted, will unfetter rather than throttle the growth of our souls. Tackling the Ten will liberate us from our *Mitzrayim*! After all, don't we mortals yearn to complete our earthly excursions as free, forgiven, and fulfilled as possible, even if not reaching any Promised Land? It will surely be enough for us, as it was for our brother Moses, to receive a soft, gentle kiss from Yahweh, when we die!

Clearly, these 10 essentials are difficult and demanding, but they're exceedingly addressable. As Deuteronomy 30:11-14 encourages:

> *For the Commandment that I give you this day—it is neither beyond you nor is it far away. It is very near to you, on your lips and in your heart, that you may do it.*

Yes, we can creatively and caringly attend to each and every one of the Ten. We liberals would be wise to excavate green and ripe discoveries from classically "conservative" documents such as the Ten Commandments. We can "hold to the difficult" (Rilke); we can do hard. And when we stumble, we can be forgiven; then get back up and keep on tackling the Ten anew.

Upon encountering the burning bush, Moses asks God for God's moniker, but the latter only responds with *Eheyeh-Asher-Eheyeh*, which is oft-rendered by the inert English, "I am who I am." The phrase more aptly translates: "I will be who I will be *or* I am becoming as I am becoming." (Exodus 3:14) Hence, God is an unfinished being, and so are we earthlings, who were, after all, created in God's likeness.

I grew up thinking that the term *Amen* meant "so be it," as if we were merely adding an exclamation point to what had just been spoken or sung in community. I've since learned that *Amen* more correctly translates as "so might it be." *Amen* refers not to an actuality so much as to our aim. *Amen* is an aspiration.

Therefore, whenever we voice an *Amen* in private or public, we're, in effect, pledging to help our sentiments and convictions come true. *Amen* is not another sweet, superfluous four-letter word thrown in for magical measure. *Amen* is a promise to translate our hopes into deeds that heal and empower the cosmos we cradle in common.

As we *Amen*-ers wrestle with the Ten Commandments, right now in 2025, my own progressive heritage delivers an eye-opening reminder. Unitarian religion is rooted in the 16th century Latin phrase of our forebears: *semper reformanda*, which denotes "always evolving." Membership in a responsibly free faith enables us to stay current and fluid as we exegete, then embody, the priorities of our journey.

A couple footnotes to this foundational phrase: *semper reformanda*. First, the overall context references both the active and passive voices. Our Transylvanian ancestors challenge us to be willing to change our external reality as well as be changed internally. And, as we all know, the tougher task is usually altering our inner realm. This historical imperative summons us to be bilateral.

Second, note the Latin word literally means *reform* which challenges us to improve our lives not just adapt or coast. *Reformanda* demands changing for the better, all our days and nights. If we stay awake and purposive, we will evolve all the way to the crypt. Rabbi David Wolpe (1958-) recaps: "Being formed in the image of God means that there is in us the infinite capacity for growth and that we will never exhaust our ability to stretch ourselves spiritually."

In truth, transformation is our explicit assignment while dwelling on earth. Our *raison d'etre* is evolution. We're summoned to stay growing to our earthly completion ... sucking life dry of its juices and richness.

The phrase that keeps echoing in my soul is "never too late." "Never too late, never too late, Tom!" Hence, as long as I'm breathing, I vow to keep my heart cavernous and my mind stirring ... fully aware that my achievements will rarely match my aspirations. "Tenderly yet resolutely onward" has become my operational mantra.

Consequently, since my cherished Carolyn's death, after forty-six years of residing in our beautiful San Diego domicile, I've moved to Santa Barbara to optimize a fresh identity and to thicken bonds with the portion of my family who least know my smell.

Despite inevitable surprises, yea complications and vexations, my relocation has proven to be the right choice at the right time for the right reasons.

I'm venturing novel ways of dwelling in my current universe. For example, I've been entering the doorway of a Buddhist sangha and signing on. As an utter novice, I'm beginning to eat more gratefully and mindfully, tabling my utensil after each bite, and, most of all, aspiring to consume with profounder respect toward all living beings. Brother Phap Linh nudges me wisely:

> *When eating a piece of broccoli, or a spoonful of rice, we have an opportunity to directly experience our interconnection with the entire cosmos. We have a chance to taste the radiant sunlight, the bounteous earth, the wandering moon, and the softness of rain. This is not mere intellectual understanding; it's living insight.*

I'm strolling more reflectively, instead of racing off to my next task or destination. I'm aspiring to make each physical step, emotional choice, and relational connection a peaceful one. In fact, I will shortly be receiving the Transmission of the Five Mindfulness Trainings (administered through Thich Nhat Hanh's Plum Village tradition) as well as given a Dharma name...a process, which, in profound ways, resembles and reinforces our mission of wrestling with the Decalogue. To be sure, I'm stumbling and wobbling amidst my path of engaged Buddhism, but I reduce self-pressure and skirt external scorecards remembering that "right diligence is a blend of effort and ease."

And my entrance into a local recovery program (supporting family and friends suffering from alcoholism) in Santa Barbara has encouraged me to cease "noble" attempts to set the agendas of others or to fix their problems ... and instead to labor on my own psycho-social-spiritual development. My recovering also helps moderate my being a perennial "people-pleaser" and "recognition-seeker" and propels me toward a healthier and more responsible earthly conclusion. My latest endeavors have proven to be both soothing and stretching, albeit uncomfortable. But, as my colleague, Alma Crawford, reminds: "Discomfort is a spiritual discipline."

Everything I am, say, or do is becoming an occasion for soulful practice. My present moments are tumbling forth as teachable ones.

Semper reformanda ...

Nonetheless, remember, my fellow pilgrims, we're seeking progress not perfection during our lifetimes, since the latter is an unrealizable goal, even when you think of it in terms of eons and eons. Gutzon Borglum (1867-1941), the sculptor who created the massive Mount Rushmore Memorial, was once asked if he considered his work perfect in detail. "Not today," he replied. "The nose of Washington is an inch too long. It's better that way, though, because it'll erode to be approximately right in about 10,000 years." Note, Borglum said "approximately right!"

And, of course, only imperfect heart beats keep us alive. Cardiologists are discovering that the heart approaches a perfect symmetry and balance only a few hours before we die. Therefore, as we humans serve and cry, quarrel and dance, our hearts always pulse with a slightly irregular rhythm.

One of my beloved Hebraic scriptures on maintaining an evergreen awareness is Psalm 91:14: "In old age they still produce fruit; they are always green and full of sap." Our final laps should, in fact, be generative ones, "always green and full of sap," at least, sufficiently green and oozing with sap. Still relevant and sprouting all the way to our grave.

So, I've struggled to keep on advancing from a little boy—graced by my mother with pen and paper—into an elder, still writing and aspiring to ensoul a greener rendition of my original incarnation.

Wrestling freshly and unceasingly with the Ten Commandments has assisted me in completing my life in a more honest and honorable manner.

May it do the same for you.

Afterword

"The more we embrace life with justice, compassion, curiosity, awe, wonder, serenity, and humility, the more we become aware of God in, with, and as all things."
—Rami M. Shapiro

As Tom Owen-Towle's book so beautifully demonstrates, Moses's Ten Sayings are open to interpretation from generation to generation.

I have been a student of Zen Buddhism even longer than I have been a rabbi. Many decades ago, I received a request from a group of Jews living at Plum Village, Thich Nhat Hanh's Zen Center in southwest France. The recitation of vows was part of Plum Village's daily practice, and I was asked to create a set of "Jewish vows" that could be added by those who felt the need to do so. I turned to Moses's Ten Sayings, adapting the biblical text to the Plum Village format of "Aware of the suffering caused by…"

SPIRITUALITY IS A SOURCE OF LIBERATION

Aware of the suffering caused by enslavement to things and ideas, I vow to liberate myself from all addictions and compulsive behaviors, both material and spiritual.

GOD CANNOT BE NAMED

Aware of the suffering caused by gods crafted in my own image for my own profit, I vow to acknowledge all ideas of God as human constructs, shaped by history and circumstance, and perpetually unable to define Reality.

GOD CANNOT BE OWNED

Aware of the suffering caused by the misuse of God and religion in the pursuit of power, I vow to free myself from all ideologies that demonize others, and to honor only those teachings that uphold the freedom and dignity of women, men, and nature.

REMEMBER THE SABBATH

Aware of the suffering caused by an excessive attachment to work, consumption, and technology, I vow to set aside a Sabbath for personal freedom, creativity, and play.

HONORING THE AGED

Aware of the suffering caused by old age, I vow to care for my parents to the best of my ability and promote the dignity and well-being of all elderly people.

DO NOT MURDER

Aware of the suffering caused by violence, I vow to cultivate gentleness in all my actions.

AVOID SEXUAL MISCONDUCT

Aware of the suffering caused by sexual exploitation, I vow never to degrade another through irresponsible or deceitful use of sexuality.

DO NOT STEAL

Aware of the suffering caused by injustice, theft, and oppression, I vow to respect the property of others, promote the fair sharing of resources, and cultivate generosity within myself and my community.

DO NOT LIE

Aware of the suffering caused by hurtful speech, I vow to speak truthfully and compassionately, avoiding gossip, slander, and discordant speech.

DO NOT COVET

Aware of the suffering caused by endless desire, I vow to live simply, to avoid debt, and to own only that which brings me joy.

While I make no pretense to keeping these vows with anything approaching perfection, I have found them to personalize the Ten Commandments for daily practice. I hope sharing them with you here strengthens the impact of Tom Owen-Towle's fine book, as you aspire to live with purpose and integrity in crafting your own interpretation of the Ten Sayings.

Rabbi Rami Shapiro, Ph.D.
Rabbi Shapiro is an award-winning author of nearly forty books on religion, spirituality, and recovery. His most recent book is titled: *Zen Mind—Jewish Mind* (2025).

About the Author

Tom Owen-Towle is entering his 58th year of ordained ministry and is the author of two dozen books on personal relationships, social justice work, and spiritual growth. Tom is a guitarist and parlor magician who, in what he calls his "re-firement" years, sings in nursing homes, mentors youth, and volunteers at the local homeless center. Owen-Towle also lectures and conducts workshops on Conscious Aging and Mindful Dying.

Rev. Owen-Towle has dedicated this book to his wife of 50 years, Carolyn, who died in 2023, amidst its very creation. She soulfully embodied the vision Tom shares in *Living with Purpose and Integrity: A Fresh Perspective on the Ten Commandments*.

www.ingramcontent.com/pod-product-compliance
Lightning Source LLC
Chambersburg PA
CBHW031625160426
43196CB00006B/289